Art That Works

Art That Works

*The Decorative
Arts of the Eighties,
Crafted in America*

Lloyd E. Herman

University of Washington Press *Seattle & London*

Copyright © 1990 by Lloyd E. Herman

Composition by the Department of Printing, University
of Washington
Printed and bound by Dai Nippon Printing Company, Tokyo
Designed by Audrey Meyer

Library of Congress Cataloging in Publication Data

Herman, Lloyd E.
    Art that works: the decorative arts of the eighties, crafted
in America / Lloyd E. Herman.
        p. cm.
    ISBN 0-295-96937-7 (alk. paper) ISBN 0-295-97007-3 (pbk.)
    1. Decorative arts–United States–History–20th century–
Themes, motives. I. Title.
    NK808.H43   1990
    745'.0973'07473–dc20   89-39843
                                                    CIP

The paper used in this publication meets the minimum
requirements of the American National Standard for Information
Sciences—Permanence of Paper for Printed Library Materials,
ANSI Z39.48-1984

Frontispiece: **Michael K. Speaker**
Red River Steer Desk (See also plate 32)

Exhibition Schedule

This book has been published on the occasion of the exhibition,
Art That Works: The Decorative Arts of the Eighties, Crafted in America,
organized and circulated by Art Services International, Alexandria,
Virginia. As of the time of publication, the exhibition schedule follows:

Mint Museum of Art, Charlotte, North Carolina
August 19–October 7, 1990

Huntsville Museum of Art, Huntsville, Alabama
November 17, 1990–January 13, 1991

Albany Institute of History and Art, Albany, New York
February 2–March 31, 1991

Minnesota Museum of Art, St. Paul, Minnesota
April 20–June 16, 1991

Philbrook Museum of Art, Tulsa, Oklahoma
July 6–September 1, 1991

Birmingham Museum of Art, Birmingham, Alabama
September 21–November 17, 1991

DeCordova and Dana Museum, Lincoln, Massachusetts
December 7, 1991–February 2, 1992

Dayton Art Institute, Dayton, Ohio
February 22–April 19, 1992

Arkansas Art Center, Little Rock, Arkansas
May 9–July 5, 1992

Hunter Museum of Art, Chattanooga, Tennessee
July 25–September 20, 1992

Portland Art Museum, Portland, Maine
October 10–December 6, 1992

Lowe Art Museum, Coral Gables, Florida
January 2–March 28, 1993

Columbus Museum of Art, Columbus, Georgia
April 17–June 13, 1993

Delaware Art Museum, Wilmington, Delaware
July 3–August 29, 1993

Contents

Foreword

IT IS WITH GREAT PLEASURE that Art Services International presents this important exhibition—the first to highlight American decorative arts of this decade. While America's craftspeople were made virtually obsolete by the Industrial Revolution, this exhibition illustrates that they are once again producing sophisticated, even luxurious objects that will undoubtedly become the heirlooms of tomorrow. Through the presentations of *Art That Works: The Decorative Arts of the Eighties, Crafted in America,* our goal is to enhance the understanding and enjoyment of contemporary American decorative arts.

The organization of an exhibition of this scope and complexity has necessarily spanned several years and involved many individuals. In particular, Art Services International is indebted to Lloyd E. Herman, founding director of the Smithsonian Institution's Renwick Gallery. Mr. Herman conceived of the exhibition and has worked closely with ASI throughout its development. We very much value his expertise and are honored to have collaborated with him on this important project.

We are also most grateful to the directors and staff of the museums participating in the tour for giving us their enthusiastic support and cooperation. We are delighted to be able to assist so many of our finest institutions across the country in bringing *Art That Works* to their communities.

As always, the key to the success of any exhibition tour is the generosity of the lenders, and we are indebted to the many collectors and artists who ultimately made this tour possible. Their willingness to part with these key works is especially gratifying and, through the exhibition and catalogue, their generosity will enrich the lives of thousands.

We wish to thank The Andrew W. Mellon Foundation, notably Executive Vice-President Neil Rudenstine, for their continued funding of our catalogue program. In addition we would like to express our sincere thanks to the staff of Art Services International, particularly Erica C. Hennig, Elizabeth A. Hooper, and Sally Thomas, who have patiently attended to the many practical details of the tour.

Facing page: **Komelia Hongja Okim**
Mountain-Scape II (See also plate 81)

Lynn Kahler Berg and Joseph W. Saunders
Directors, Art Services International

Preface

IN THE FIFTEEN YEARS I directed the national craft museum of the United States—the Smithsonian's Renwick Gallery in Washington, D.C.—I watched the modern craft movement grow and diversify. Our national competition for production craftspeople in 1975 resulted in the nationwide traveling exhibition, *Craft Multiples*. That exhibition brought attention to the makers of well-designed functional objects in series, at a time when the unique artistic creation in clay, metal, wood, glass, or fiber was strongly emphasized. Not all of the artists whose work was included had found labor-saving ways to replicate their designs using production methods, but that soon changed. The successful wholesale/retail craft fairs initiated by the American Craft Council quickly demonstrated that there was a vast market in America for quality crafts, but wholesale buyers for stores insisted on a consistency of product.

Since then, many potters have adopted slip casting to reproduce identical shapes in clay, furniture makers have used templates to cut like parts, and metalsmiths have bought preformed or precolored elements for use in their metal objects. Production crafts have become highly visible reminders of a time-honored craft tradition—making objects for use.

Multiples of a single crafted design may be made today as in the past with hand tools and natural materials. But it is just as likely that today's university-educated craftsperson will use plastic resins, or refractory metals from the space program, in an object. Techniques may incorporate borrowed traditions—Asian methods of dyeing or metal inlay; European processes of wood marquetry—or innovative applications of computer assistance in formulating ceramic glazes or weave patterns.

The modern craftsperson in America, unhampered by a single strong craft tradition, has the world as a textbook. The inspiration of graphics and colors in 1950s advertising, traditional African carving, eighteenth-century English furniture—all may simultaneously infuse modern works with verve. The "re" decade of the 1980s, so dubbed by *Esquire* magazine because of its rampant style-revivalism led by Post Modernism in architecture, is no less so for America's craftworkers.

This book complements and documents an exhibition of the same name. From the thousands of American craftspeople who practice as artists, I have selected the work of 112. Their objects, transmuting ideas and elements drawn from the past or from other cultures, exemplify the sophistication of style and workmanship prevalent in American crafts today.

Art Services International (ASI) of Alexandria, Virginia, has organized the traveling exhibition and arranged for its circulation. I am grateful to ASI's codirectors, Lynn Kahler Berg and Joseph W. Saunders, for their enthusiastic support of the project. I value especially my many friends in the crafts community, and I am particularly grateful to these artists themselves for their help and cooperation.

Lloyd E. Herman

Facing page: **Anthony Giachetti**
Fluted Cabinet #882 (detail) (See also plate 10)

Study of an interior by C. W. Clark, from *The Decorator and Furnisher*, April 1888. *Library of Congress photograph*

Art That Works

AMERICAN CRAFTS aren't what they used to be. Hand-made things are no longer necessary to furnish our homes or to clothe our bodies. Machines make our necessities today. In the past 100 years American crafts have matured and grown sophisticated, moving from the popular perception of rustic chairs, brown bean-pots, and colorful quilts to objects of great technical virtuosity and expressive power—as stylish as decorative arts from any place or period in museum collections.

Note that term—"decorative art." Scorned by modern craftsmen as connoting frivolous, unnecessary decoration on functional objects, its use has been revived in the 1980s. The term, never abandoned by museums and historians, today describes utilitarian household objects that go beyond the merely functional. The best of these home furnishings add verve and originality to utility. They are a vital element of America's visual arts in this century. They are art—art that works, as well as art that is beautiful.

Many people are puzzled, if not downright alienated, by much contemporary art. The aesthetic challenges raised by today's "fine" arts—painting, sculpture, drawing, and printmaking—are beyond many of us who want to be surrounded by things of beauty. Artists using craft materials and techniques may also make objects that provoke and question, eschewing utilitarian tradition to be purely expressive. But America's craftspeople haven't abandoned beauty. Far from it. The decorative arts of the eighties are colorful, richly textured, elegant in surface and form. They wed down-to-earth utility with high-style sheen. They are the new heirlooms—to be used, but preserved for future generations.

A Century of American Crafts

During the last 100 years American crafts have changed, yet in many ways have remained the same. Let us look at the 1880s, then stride briskly through nine decades to review what the 1980s are all about.

In the second half of the last century, English and American craftspeople were losing ground to industry.

Factories were churning out furniture, silverplate, ceramic statues, and other extravagantly embellished goods for the home. It was a time of showmanship for the machine. The printed fabrics and wallpapers, the carved and embossed wood furniture, the molded and painted ceramic figurines and tablewares were as busy with ornament as they could be. Unfortunately, many were grossly overdecorated or were embellished in inappropriate ways. It was a period of excess.

But along with the excesses of the 1880s and nineties were works by significant designers who drew on other times for their inspiration. The Philadelphia Centennial Exhibition of 1876 revived America's patriotic fervor and extolled our colonial heritage. Soon there were Victorian adaptations of colonial styles, and the spinning wheel—an anachronism in the 1880s—became a decorative parlor reminder of the past. Other styles were revived, often with the exaggeration we associate with Victorian pomposity. These included the Rococo, Gothic, Renaissance, exotic Asian, Egyptian, and Neo-Grec. Such exuberant fantasies were not limited to high-style expensive furniture, but were found in mass-produced goods, affordable to the growing middle class.

The Arts and Crafts Movement

In England, reaction to the garish design excesses and shoddy workmanship of the new manufactured housewares was led by social reformer John Ruskin and his disciple William Morris. In founding the Arts and Crafts movement, Ruskin and Morris strove to return dignity to handcraftsmanship, emphasizing an improved way of life and improved products. As the movement crested in England, an American wave followed. But as craft historian Edward Lucie-Smith has observed in *Craft Today: Poetry of the Physical*, the American Arts and Crafts movement was often negative, rejecting the dominance of industry, rather than positive, as in England, stressing revival of hand skills.

A craftsman living room, with tiled fireplace and window seats,
from *The Craftsman*, October 1905. *Library of Congress photograph*

The Arts and Crafts movement in America was not characterized by a single, dominant modern style. It incorporated strains of Art Nouveau, the French adaptation of Japanese style linked to the Aesthetic movement in England and America, the direct Japanese influence seen in the designs of Henry Mather Greene and Charles Sumner Greene, and the rectilinear style of Scottish architect/designer, Charles Rennie Mackintosh. Gustav Stickley, a leading Arts and Crafts furniture maker, gave the movement voice through publication of *The Craftsman*.

Arts and Crafts societies sprang up in numerous American cities, and exhibitions gave visibility to the new artistic products. Designs emphasized simplicity of form and naturalized decoration—usually flowers and plants represented realistically or gently stylized. Ceramics often had subtle matte surfaces; greens and soft natural colors seemed to predominate over the strong reds and purples and the gilded adornments of popular manufactured wares.

Honesty of workmanship was prized not only in household furnishings but in houses designed for those who subscribed to the crafts philosophy. The architecture and furnishings designed by Henry Mather Greene and Charles Sumner Greene exemplified this—even making a fetish of beams joined with wood pegs (some only covering screw heads) and of essential joinery exposed for decorative effect. Objects were made in studios by individuals or in small factories that provided dignified work opportunities for young women with artistic talent. The art potteries of the late nineteenth and early twentieth centuries employed men to throw the pots, and women to decorate them. One prominent woman ceramist, Adelaide Alsop Robineau, not only carved intricate designs into her porcelain vases but helped to unite ceramics with the Arts and Crafts movement by publishing the journal *Keramic Studio*, beginning in 1899. Robineau, Maria Longworth Nichols (who founded the Rookwood Pottery), and the American art potteries were instrumental in establishing an American Arts and Crafts style.

Also influential was Englishman Charles Fergus Binns, who was hired in 1900 to originate the curriculum at the New York State School of Clayworking and Ceramics at Alfred University. Binns's models for ceramic form were not from England's Arts and Crafts movement, but from the classic forms of Chinese, Greek, and Persian pots. It is reported that he taught his students to use jiggers to ensure that the curves and proportions matched those of the prototypes—perhaps leading the way to the yet-to-come profession of industrial design.

Though Robineau was in New York State, as were Gustav Stickley and his brothers, Leopold and George, the art potteries were found mostly in Ohio. The movement was not an eastern phenomenon. Two southern California architects, the Greene brothers, designed the innovative California bungalow as well as the furnishings for those houses they built for wealthy clients. Arthur and Lucia Mathews, working in the San Francisco Bay area, designed furniture, picture frames, and decorative objects that not only made historical reference but were usually decorated with the native flowers of California.

Ironically, the movement—though conceived to produce well-designed, well-made household goods for the masses as an alternative to garish manufactured stuff—never reached a mass market. Then, as now, the masses wanted what they think rich people own. The Arts and Crafts movement was embraced by a minority who respected the handmade and who espoused the philosophical underpinnings of the movement. Without broad support, the movement waned. *The Craftsman* ceased publication in 1916. World War I reduced the availability of precious metals and some other craft materials. Furthermore, patriotism for the war effort made purchase of luxuries unfashionable. The movement petered out before the 1920s.

The American Craft Heritage

Not all American craftsmen were allied with the Arts and Crafts movement. Far from it. Folk crafts in rural America have survived from the colonial era, diversifying with successive waves of European immigration. Though manufactured goods replaced handmade products of many kinds, people who revered our craft heritage found ways to help preserve it. For example, in the early 1900s a few weavers took steps to preserve the tradition of coverlet-weaving, which had been supplanted by machine-woven goods. They introduced coarser yarns and tried other methods to reduce weaving time and labor. Others, seeing the end to that tradition, recorded patterns and "weave recipes." To preserve colonial furniture styles, the Reverend Wallace Nutting produced high-quality replicas of what he dubbed "pilgrim" furniture, advocating its appropriateness to American idealism in the young century. Medieval decorative designs in forged iron were adapted by Philadelphian Samuel Yellin, who won commissions in various cities to design and fabricate handsome iron grilles, screens, and gates for buildings. Louis Comfort Tiffany, fueled by the success of his art glass, introduced his ceramics at the St. Louis Exposition in 1904, at the same time that Englishman Frederick Carder founded the Steuben Glass Works in Corning, New York. Their rivalry over similar iridescent glass surfaces led to a lawsuit and, eventually, to friendship. It is important to remember, though, that Tiffany was primarily an artist directing skilled technicians to realize his creations, while Carder was an inveterate inventor-researcher who applied his discoveries (and rediscoveries) to a wide range of beautiful, functional glass objects—also made in multiples in a factory.

LITTLE HAS BEEN recorded about American crafts between the two world wars, except in ceramics, but no evidence has been cited that a major stylistic influence or movement united American craftspeople. The 1920s brought recognition to native American crafts and folk art from interested artists and collectors. Native American potter Maria Martinez, of San Ildefonso Pueblo in New Mexico, working with her husband Julian, rediscovered the secret of the black-on-black pottery that brought fame to their pueblo.

Also in the late 1920s, Wharton Esherick, dean of American furniture craftsmen by midcentury, exerted a distinctive Art Deco influence on furniture design, working from his studio in Paoli, Pennsylvania (now the Wharton Esherick Museum). The Art Deco style, so named for the International Exposition of Decorative Arts in Paris in 1925, was not strongly felt in the United States until the 1930s, when it—like the earlier "mission" furniture style of the Arts and Crafts movement—was copied by manufacturers. The influence of the 1930s on ceramics was not purely Art Deco. It also had strong links to the Wiener Werkstatte—to Vienna as the Bauhaus was to Germany—the exemplar of modern style. In America, the Werkstatte's influence was most strongly felt in Cleveland, Ohio, where artists who had studied in Vienna infused their ceramic sculpture with European style and wit.

Among the handful of ceramists active in the 1930s in Cleveland, Edris Eckhardt and Viktor Schreckengost are still creating/designing more than fifty years later. During the thirties, Eckhardt was strongly associated with the Work Projects Administration (WPA), a federal government program to provide diversified employment during the Depression. For artists, the WPA's Federal Art Project involved crafts and craftspeople across the nation. In Oregon, WPA artists designed and made furnishings and decorations for Timberline Lodge on Mt. Hood, weaving draperies, bedspreads, and rugs for the guest bedrooms; designing, constructing, and carving furniture; forging decorative gates and fireplace fittings; creating wood mosaics and other ornamental surfaces for public rooms.

In New York State, Seneca Indians were employed to re-create objects of the Iroquois culture. In Connecticut, the WPA sponsored a toy-making project. And in Cleveland, where Eckhardt directed a WPA office, artists made handcrafted furniture, fabrics, and playground sculpture. Eckhardt herself created a series of figurines depicting familiar storybook characters, which were replicated and distributed to public libraries to encourage reading.

Another major WPA effort was the Index of American Design. Artists painted meticulous watercolor "portraits" of American crafts and folk arts from the colonial era through the end of the nineteenth century. These 16,000 images, housed in the National Gallery of Art in Washington, D.C., provide both a reminder of America's craft history and a design inspiration to craftmakers today.

The household necessities made by rural craftsmen probably helped to sustain them during the Depression, even though money for nonessentials was short. But in 1939, Allan Eaton's rural American crafts research was published in *Crafts of the Southern Highlands.* It validated the crafts of that region and helped to renew interest in them. It was followed in 1946 by his *Crafts of New England.* Both books remain valuable references to craftmaking in this era. They served to revive the pride of craftmakers in their work and to bring the attention of others to an important part of their American heritage, as did the Index of American Design. Exhibitions of regional crafts and other forms of attention soon followed. Both the Southern Highlands Handicraft Guild and the New Hampshire League of Craftsmen were founded in the 1930s. They remain vital today in promoting crafts in their regions.

The European Craft Influence

It is easy to characterize the Depression as only a time of deprivation, when few had the luxury of making or buying handmade goods. But American crafts were being invigorated, both by a growing reverence for a national craft heritage and also by a new perspective on craftmaking and craft education brought by recent European refugees and immigrants.

The sophisticated art objects made by craftsmen immigrating from Europe were at the other extreme from American vernacular and folk crafts. The threat of Naziism brought Jewish craftspeople to the United States to make new lives. Austrian ceramists Gertrud and Otto Natzler settled in Los Angeles. They won their first award in 1938 at the Syracuse Ceramic National Exhibition—a series that, for decades, recorded the best of American ceramics.

Trude Guermonprez, an Austrian weaver, established a studio in northern California, as did potters Frans and Marguerite Wildenhain, from Holland and Germany, respectively. Marguerite, educated at the Bauhaus, had been a respected ceramic designer in Germany. She was revered by many as a "potter's potter" until her death in the 1980s. When the Bauhaus closed, Anni and Josef Albers—neither speaking English—came from Germany to join the faculty of the experimental Black Mountain College in North Carolina.

Not all European immigrants came to escape Naziism, however. For example, George G. Booth, a newspaper publisher from Detroit, and his wife Ellen founded Cranbrook Academy of Art in Bloomfield Hills, Michigan. They attracted the renowned Finnish architect Eliel Saarinen as its first director in 1930. Other European craftspeople formed the first faculty: Marianne Strengel, who directed the textiles program, and Maija Grotell, head of ceramics, were Finnish artist/teachers who influenced generations of American craftspeople. Arthur Nevill Kirk, an English goldsmith, brought to America the "Liberty's look," a somewhat Scandinavianized Art Deco style popularized by the Liberty department store in London. In fact, the entire Cranbrook campus, with buildings designed by Eliel Saarinen and sculpture by Swedish-born Carl Milles, continues to exemplify a distinctive thirties style, just as Cranbrook remains one of the most important educational institutions for modern American craftspeople.

TO SUMMARIZE THE 1930s, the decade reaffirmed the importance of America's traditional crafts. In addition, the nation's new immigrants provided fresh viewpoints on artistic style and craft education that would exert a lasting influence. The establishment of various craft organizations helped members start to publicize and market their work. WPA programs gave crafts visibility and helped to establish a place for craftspeople, including in architecture.

The 1940s

Crafts declined as an occupational choice during the 1940s while the nation was at war, but the war's end signaled a new era for American crafts. Metal holloware techniques were disseminated by a series of workshops for metalworking teachers, sponsored by Handy and Harmon, a smelter/supplier of precious metals. The ripple effect generated by those few teachers, and by Margaret Craver's use of metalsmithing in rehabilitation programs for war veterans, was significant.

Perhaps of greatest importance was the availability of increased educational opportunity for veterans through the G.I. Bill. Veterans could return to school to earn university degrees subsidized by the United States Government. To serve their needs, universities expanded their curricula. Many added art and craft courses that were attractive to new students with a mature outlook on their futures.

The 1950s

Craftspeople who had worked in relative isolation in previous decades began to find a common voice in the 1950s through the American Craftsmen's Cooperative Council (now the American Craft Council or ACC). The first national craft conference, a nationally circulated publication, and a museum in New York all were sponsored by the ACC. These membership services provided the first national network linking craftspeople with their fellow artists. It opened doors nationwide to exchange of technical information and stylistic influences.

While craftmakers were caught up in the general spirit of optimism and economic growth in the 1950s, their objects remained tied to functional usage. A fully expressive art was found mainly in such traditional narrative and decorative works as tapestries and stained-glass windows. Modernism, however, was very much in vogue. New forms abounded in every medium, though the materials, and techniques used to manipulate them, were far more limited than they are today.

The principal media for modern expression were clay and fiber. Clay forms were, for the most part, wheel thrown, and textiles were woven. The exceptions were notable and influential. The Abstract Expressionist movement in painting gained a position in the craft world through such craft artists as Mariska Karacz, whose abstract forms in stitchery had wide visibility via a national magazine, and Peter Voulkos, who taught ceramics at the Otis Art Institute and later at the University of California, Berkeley. Lenore Tawney hung her loom-woven hangings away from the wall, creating see-through fiber sculpture. Margaret DePatta veered from tradition in jewelry making, choosing eccentrically cut gems or smooth river pebbles to combine as separate elements in her sculptural brooches. John Paul Miller looked to the past to revive the ancient art of granulation, but the jewelry forms to which he applied the tiny gold spheres were definitely modern.

The 1960s

Looking forward, and looking back, became more apparent in the 1960s. A period of great social unrest in the nation, the decade polarized the nation with grave issues such as the war in Vietnam, the civil rights movement in the South, and the assassination of political leaders. Many young people, alienated by big business and an unsympathetic government, chose the simpler life of rural America, where they believed they could survive by selling homegrown vegetables and homemade crafts by the roadside or at local craft fairs. Macramé plant hangers and tie-dyed T-shirts characterized these do-it-yourself crafts. Unfortunately, the mediocre quality of many objects made and sold undermined wide acceptance of the university-educated craftmakers as artists.

These same craftmakers struggled to prove that an artist's expressive possibilities were not limited to paint and canvas. Many of the amateurs became skilled at marketing, refining their technical expertise to complement their design talents. But many of the decade's dropouts did not become commercially successful craftsmen. Could it be that those who had taken the academic road to their crafts profession then used the sixties to redirect their energies and to seek new inspiration? The 1960s, building on the acceptance of modern craft styles in the 1950s, nurtured the freedom to experiment. Many craftspeople explored Asian religions, finding sustenance for their souls while adapting techniques and materials from various foreign cultures to their own craft uses. The Peace Corps, Fulbright Fellowships, and other international programs provided living opportunities abroad. And at home, a multitude of influences—international, social, and political—provided inspiration for artists in contemporary craft. An emphasis on content, and an independence from functional craft traditions, separated the new craft artists from those who made utilitarian objects.

The sixties can be characterized in several other ways; the ceramics and textile fields were especially affected. An off-handed—sometimes outrageous—humor characterized the "funk" movement in ceramics emanating from the San Francisco Bay area and exemplified by Robert Arneson. The exploration of familiar textile techniques, such as knitting and crochet, and more exotic techniques, such as Scandinavian card-weaving, knotless netting from New Guinea, weaving methods from ancient Peru, and pile rug-making from Finland, as well as the introduction of such untraditional weaving materials as plastic and newspapers all found credibility in the 1960s.

THE INTERNATIONAL tapestry biennials, first held in Lausanne, Switzerland, in 1963, provided an international focus on large-scale sculptural fiber art. As much prominence as the new "art fabric" received in the 1960s, textile art of the period cannot be characterized easily. The homespun affectations of society's drop-outs embraced the quilt as their medium and renewed its vigor. "Soft sculpture" was added to the textile lexicon, and the term applied both to the new off-loom woven sculptures and to padded fabric constructions. The aforementioned macramé and the equally popular tie-dyed fabrics were so ubiquitous that they came to characterize the counterculture of the decade.

In 1962, Harvey Littleton, a ceramist from Wisconsin, and Dominick Labino, a glass engineer in Ohio, conducted a workshop at the Toledo (Ohio) Museum of Art. There they introduced to artists the possibilities offered by a small glass furnace for studio use. Labino brought glass marbles made from a formula that artists could melt easily. Within the decade, that workshop led to the formation of glassblowing programs in more than 100 art schools and universities. Glass moved out of the factory and into the art studio.

The 1970s

The freedom to explore technique and material was not lost in the 1970s. Indeed, the impetus for exploration and investigation of technique and material grew and grew. Jewelers, led by Stanley Lechtzin, a teacher at the Tyler School of Art in Philadelphia, experimented with electroforming. By this method, commonly used to bronze baby shoes, artists could build up thin films of metal on virtually any surface, creating the appearance of massive, organic jewelry that was very light in weight. A landmark workshop in 1970 at Southern Illinois University at Carbondale introduced traditional blacksmithing to jewelers and other metalsmiths. That workshop, organized by Professor L. Brent Kington, revived the use of iron-forging techniques in creating architectural ornamentation as well as tables, plantstands, torchères, and so forth.

And, just as iron forged by young makers like Kington and Albert Paley began to find its way into the world of art, so basketry was explored for the expressive potential of various rigid structural forms. Felting and hand papermaking were also investigated for their artistic possibilities and were popularized through informal workshops. They were added, as well, to the curricula of the crafts schools. Handcrafted clothing moved away from the shapeless poncho of the 1960s and closer to *haute couture*, as the "wearable art" movement developed momentum and as craftspeople, specializing in textile techniques, expressed themselves in theatrical, humorous, or style-conscious clothing. Related to the creation of such artistic clothing was the "surface design" movement, which compelled fiber artists to examine the expressive uses of pattern and color on fabric surfaces. Painting, printing, and dyeing took their places in the catalogue of acceptable textile techniques, along with color Xerography, heat transfer of photographic images, and numerous dyeing techniques borrowed from Asia—*batik, ikat,* and *plange,* to name a few. Appliquéd and pieced quilts, beading, stitchery, and other surface embellishments were all accepted as part of this fledgling movement, which soon boasted a membership organization and a publication.

Organizations and publications were, in fact, part of the growing network of information available to the crafts community in the 1970s. *Surface Design Journal, Fiberarts, Fine Woodworking, Metalsmith,* and *The Bead Journal* (now *Ornament*) all began publishing in the 1970s. Craft artists formed new organizations and began to hold conferences to share their mutual need for information, supplementing the American Craft Council (ACC) as the only national voice for America's craftspeople. The Society of North American Goldsmiths (SNAG), the Glass Art Society (GAS), the National Council on Education in the Ceramic Arts (NCECA), and the Artist Blacksmith Association of North America (ABANA) continue today, with even more specialized organizations representing enamelists, quilt-makers, and wood-turners joining the throng. All have been instrumental in the development of diverse techniques, permitting practitioners to expand their technical vocabularies in the service of ideas.

Ideas, content, meaning—all were important to craftspeople in the 1970s. The door into the art world was wedged open in the 1960s and was given high visibility when the landmark exhibition, *Objects: USA,* premiered in 1969. That nationally selected exhibition traveled across the United States and the world through the late 1960s and early 1970s. It provided an eye-filling array of handcrafted objects, demonstrating the artistic potential that modern craftsmen were finding in common clay, glass, fiber, metal, and wood. Museums and galleries began to take notice. New galleries spurred development of the collector market.

Galleries were only one avenue through which craftspeople began to sell their work. The country craft fair grew into a major wholesale-retail marketing opportunity for many makers, first as the ACC's northeast regional fair grew into the nationally selected Craft Fair at Rhinebeck (NY). The Rhinebeck fair attracted buyers from high-quality gift shops and department stores and from a bur-geoning number of craft shops across the country. Their need for quantities of a single design forced craftsmen to rethink their production methods. Deadlines for deliveries had to be met. Production shortcuts or a division of labor had to be used to speed manufacture.

Other marketing opportunities presented themselves. Percent-for-art programs gave craftsmen an opportunity to humanize public buildings with ceramic murals, stained-glass windows, ornamental iron grilles, and dramatic large-scale fiber hangings. Interior designers, accustomed to directing attention in a room to an important antique, began to see that contemporary handcrafted objects could add a distinctive accent. American crafts were becoming symbols of quality and originality, whether the objects were sculptural and purely expressive or were made for use.

The 1980s: Art That Works

Because of new opportunities to sell crafts in the 1980s, today's craftspeople have had to learn business practices and marketing skills. Many have become entrepreneurs, enlarging their studios to include several employees who make or finish their original designs. Selection for booth space is highly competitive in a growing number of craft fairs—ACC's wholesale/retail fairs and nationally juried retail fairs sponsored by museums as fundraisers—and is based on submission of a slide portfolio. Craftspeople have had to hone the photographic presentation of their objects. Furthermore, to compete successfully in this widening market, they have had to become aware of fashion and market trends, improving their product designs to attract the jaded eyes of wholesale buyers and finding or creating their own niches.

Handcrafted functional goods, even those made using production shortcuts and a division of labor, can rarely compete in price with similar manufactured goods. But many American makers in the 1980s have found that by refining their designs and by creating luxurious effects through selection of fine materials and finishing qualities, they can justify their prices to consumers.

Who are these consumers? Many were craft fair shoppers in the sixties whose tastes have matured as handmade merchandise has improved. Others were wooed by craft galleries, whose owners have performed an important educational function along with museums showing contemporary crafts. Many collectors are self-made businesspeople—a notable number are real estate developers—who became interested in collecting after they became prosperous enough to afford such an indulgence. Other young professionals have indulged their interest in architecture and interior design by including the handmade among their treasured possessions.

Not that craft collecting is necessarily expensive today, but prices are definitely up. Investment potential attracts another kind of collector who had seen prices escalate for other twentieth-century decorative arts from the Arts and Crafts movement and later periods. And, unlike collectors of paintings or prints, collectors of contemporary crafts find social satisfaction and prestige in such groups as the American Craft Museum's Collectors Circle and the James Renwick Alliance. Serious collectors often also belong to, and attend conferences of, the major medium organizations such as NCECA and GAS.

The refinement of their collections has caused many collectors to seek earlier works by established makers. In addition, galleries and auction houses have begun to sell earlier works by living craft artists, thereby providing a secondary market for crafts. An element of competition among collectors adds stamina to the market: collecting the best of American crafts brings prestige and possible investment appreciation to the collector. To show off their prizes, some collectors have remodeled their homes or have built new homes to present museum-style installations. Some collectors have willed their objects to their heirs, or have assured their own recognition as collectors by donating their objects to museums.

MUSEUM COLLECTIONS in the 1980s verify to the marketplace the importance of American crafts in our nation's cultural heritage. Some museums collect contemporary crafts because their curators recognize the valid place of ceramics or glass in contemporary sculptural expression. Others link these new functional objects to the history of American—and world—decorative arts. Some collect them because of the materials from which they are made (glass, ceramic, metal). Some

art museums that have heretofore exhibited or collected crafts from exotic sources, such as Asian ceramics, or historic crafts, such as carved furniture and stained glass from the Middle Ages, have finally seen that American craftsmen are creating objects worthy of their interest. Except in conservative art museums that are unwilling to consider the artistic worth of anything but paintings, drawings, prints, and sculpture, crafts are finding a place in museum exhibition programs and collections.

All this is part of the constant, ongoing recategorization of art, which, in this century, has embraced printmaking and photography more quickly than it has the craft media. Museums, like the private collectors who may serve on their boards of trustees, are wooed by galleries that may no longer show crafts exclusively but may combine them with other art media. And, with the introduction in the 1980s of the International New Art Forms Exposition, a major retail art fair in Chicago at which major craft galleries from across the nation promote their artists, both public and private collectors have found a single marketplace for these new collectibles.

Who are these craftmakers of the 1980s, and how do they differ from their kin of the past? As a group, they are older than in the 1960s, because fewer young people are making the life-style decisions of earlier decades, preferring occupations in which earnings will be greater and more dependable. Consequently, enrollments in craft programs have dropped, and several universities and art schools have reduced or curtailed their craft curricula. Those schools that retain them are adding business and marketing courses to purely artistic disciplines to give their graduates the edge in the marketplace required of craftspeople today.

Some craftspeople have taken advantage of opportunities to design, not necessarily to make, their goods. Others have broadened their options by participating in arts/industry programs. For example, in the Kohler Company's Arts/Industry Program, ceramic artists work with skilled technicians in the company's toilet-and-sink factory to create new large-scale art objects cast in industrial porcelain. One 1980s spinoff of that program is Artist Editions—toilets and sinks decorated by artists. Other craftspeople have seized opportunities to design, and sometimes make, a limited edition object. Wendy Maruyama's Mickey Mackintosh Chair (plate 22), Barbara Bauer's Queen Conch Shell Teaset (plate 97), and Marek Cecula's Graphic Set (plate 99) are all limited editions. The

Workbench, a contemporary furniture chain store in New York, pioneered in the 1970s with an in-store gallery featuring handmade furniture; when commercial galleries began to represent furniture artists, The Workbench closed its gallery as no longer needed. Today, they offer for sale a collection of limited-production furniture by makers they had represented.

It is a cliché to say that the American craft movement has "come of age." But if the field is examined from almost any angle, American craftspeople are enjoying success. Collectors prize their products, museums exhibit and sometimes collect their work, magazines publicize them, and architects and designers provide them with commissions. And they are selling their works for increasingly large sums of money. Women are no longer working only in ceramics and fibers; they are carving and turning wood, making furniture, forging iron. Craftspeople are gaining recognition as designers and as artists. They are crossing boundaries that have ghettoized the crafts. Some have become superstars whose prices are escalating toward those for contemporary paintings.

Yet the oft-heard refrain that crafts are now accepted as art is overstated. Not all collectors or curators will pigeonhole expressive objects according to the materials from which they are made, but there still exists a definite art-curatorial bias against objects that have evolved from craft materials and techniques. Established painters may make the odd object in clay which will be seen as equal to their major work. Craftspeople are now edging across media lines. It has been interesting to observe in the 1980s that the two luminaries in the glass art field, Harvey K. Littleton and Dale Chihuly, each have produced drawings and prints to complement their glass sculptures. Some for whom clay is the medium of choice have also made prints or drawings. Established ceramists Peter Voulkos, Robert Arneson, and Michael Lucero have cast their work in bronze, perhaps identifying themselves with a more "serious" art medium.

The very term "craft" is scorned by many makers who believe it militates against their full acceptance as artists. Realizing the controversy the word arouses, the British Craft Centre in London changed its name to "Contemporary Applied Arts" in the 1980s. The major art fair representing America's premier craft galleries calls itself the "International New Art Forms Exposition." Even American Craft Enterprises (ACE), the American Craft Council's for-profit producer of five major wholesale/retail fairs, sells the slogan "Handmade in America" and soft-pedals the word "craft." British ceramist Allison Britton, speaking

the World Crafts Council conference in Australia in 1988, advocated dropping the word "craft" in favor of two terms: "art" to denote purely expressive objects, and "design" to mean objects that are utilitarian.

A small ripple of a movement, given advocacy by ceramic historian and gallery owner Garth Clark, seeks to identify makers of functional objects with the long history of the decorative arts. The argument makes sense—especially on examining historical references present in the works included in this survey.

The Decorative Arts

In many ways the 1980s can be compared with the 1880s. Both are peacetime periods of relative prosperity. In the 1880s, consumers with money could afford to ally themselves with culture and taste by acquiring objects for their homes that would identify their social aspirations. Often their consumer choices were ornate, with refined form and patterned surfaces—truly "decorative" arts. Artistic products were often made in small factories—not only by individual craftsmen.

Objects of the Arts and Crafts movement of the nineteenth century contrasted sharply with that era's highly ornamented manufactured goods for the home. But the modern craft revival since World War II has increasingly joined the mass market. In fact, some of the merchandise offered at ACE fairs is as slick and devoid of personality as are its factory-made counterparts. Today the simple, unadorned forms are more often those produced in factories, while the luxuriously inlaid and carved furnishings, or those using exotic woods with silken finishes, are made by craftspeople. Craftsmen may face competition from copycat manufacturers because their designs for functional objects are not protected by copyright. It is not uncommon for foreign entrepreneurs to buy a handmade American item and have it copied in Taiwan or Hong Kong, then to resell it for far less than its American originator can offer it. In the decades following the 1880s, Stickley's early modernist designs were also copied and offered nationwide by catalogue retailers. Craftsmen today tend to make furniture so special or complex that their markets will be small, or their designs too costly or difficult to replicate profitably. Unlike the 1880s, when crafts provided a clean-lined antidote to the garish ornament of manufactured goods, in the 1980s, American crafts offer an alternative to the often-sterile factory-made designs.

The decorative arts have become a hot commodity in retail markets. Magazines showing glossy interiors feed the market for new "looks" and styles. Craftsmen like Marek Cecula (plate 99) have learned how to keep ahead of manufacturing. In his Brooklyn ceramics factory Cecula can design an entire set of tableware, test-market it, make it, offer it for sale through retailers he serves, and even discount it and clear his inventory before a ceramic manufacturer can tool up for production of a new line. That flexibility gives today's craftspeople an edge on the competition; they are able to respond to the market with ever-new merchandise in small-factory lots.

Ceramist Dorothy Hafner (plate 107) supports her studio production of unique tableware with royalties from her production designs. Since 1982 she has adapted her original forms and surface decorations for manufacturing by the prestigious German firm, Rosenthal AG. As a potter, she understands clay's capability to take form, and she knows how to shape it. Consequently, where an industrial designer with only academic training might conceive a teapot shape on paper, have a plaster model made to see it in three dimensions, and then have an actual prototype made to see if it pours properly and handles comfortably, Hafner will not only conceive and make the full prototype to see that it works properly but will then draw and produce the plaster models needed by factory technicians for the manufactured product. Hafner is one of several contemporary artists who have found ways to accommodate industrial production. Another is David Tisdale (plates 89–93), who designs trays, bowls, flatware, and other serving utensils of anodized aluminum, and also supervises their cutting, assembly, and finishing in a small workshop in Manhattan. He and glassmaker Judy Smilow (plates 54, 55) have embarked on a joint design venture; they will only design—not manufacture—their products.

Options in Handcrafting:
New Techniques and Materials

What is handcraft? When does it become manufacture? These questions must be raised in the 1990s as lines become less distinct. Art glass was factory-made until 1962, when the development of a small glass furnace and a glass formula with a lower melting temperature made it possible for artists to blow glass in their own studios. Today, artists like Dale Chihuly just direct the blowing and forming of molten glass shapes that are made by a skilled team of technicians. It is a curious circle. "Manufactured" long ago ceased to mean "handmade"; today, "handmade" no longer means "made only by hand." No one questions furniture makers for using machine-driven saws, sanders, and other power equipment—or modern glues, for that matter. Potters are not required to build every piece by hand or to throw it on a wheel; slip-cast forms are quite acceptable, and their identical shapes satisfy retailers. Wall hangings may be woven on a computer-controlled loom, from computer-generated patterns. Clothing will surely be sewn together on an electric sewing machine, and it may be made of fabric machine-knit in the artist's studio. Among quiltmakers, perhaps only the purists will insist on hand-quilting of their patterned tops (which may be pieced on a sewing machine!).

And, as the machine has tempered what the hand had to do in former times, so new materials offer color and surface alternatives not possible before the present era. Gold and silver continue to impress us with their rich, gleaming surfaces, but anodized aluminum provides color to the serving pieces by David Tisdale (plates 89–93), and by Jean-Pierre and Carol Shannon Hsu (plates 74, 75). Komelia Hongja Okim works primarily in precious metals (plates 81, 82), but she ornaments them with a dash of titanium's color. That refractory metal, borrowed from the space program, is dull gray until electric current is applied to its surface. The thin layer of oxide produced is seen as different colors.

Patination of metal surfaces has provided other colorful opportunities to artists such as Christopher Ellison (plate 9). Other vivid modern materials include resins, used as inlays by makers such as Robert G. McKeown (plates 123, 124); or colored plastic laminates, usually associated with kitchen counters, and the dichroic glass that Steven Maslach uses for a rainbow of color in his glass compotes (plate 50). Inspiration traditionally comes to the craftsman from his materials; many examples here illustrate that it still does.

Translating the Traditions:
An Inspired Diversity

Inspiration today, however, more often comes from diverse sources. Unlike most other countries, the United

States has no single craft tradition. Consequently, American craftsmen are not limited to a single style or a prescribed way of working. Instead, they consider the world and its visual history to be fair game for their own interpretations. The degree to which each artist uses clues from the past can be easily seen, though not one person's work in this exhibit would be easily confused with his design sources. This selection does not deny the persistent taste for colonial period reproductions; the exhibit simply does not encompass reproductions.

The colonial period—especially the neoclassical Federal and Empire styles, and including Chippendale and Queen Anne—is not a major source of inspiration to modernmakers. Perhaps there is too much association with the museums' period rooms and the nation's great historic houses to tamper with those styles as Robert Venturi has done in the cartoonlike furniture he designed for production by Knoll International. But Richard Scott Newman (plate 25) has picked up the proportions and types of decoration seen in Empire styles and has reinterpreted them for today, complete with ormolu mounts. Their gilded bronze ornaments function almost like jewelry on his furniture.

John Dodd (plate 8) and Barry Yavener (plate 37) reinterpret neoclassic styles in quite different ways. Dodd simplifies a classic column and treats it as a tall pedestal that functions as a chest. And though Yavener describes his table and mirror as neo-Empire, his silver sword ornaments also recall Art Deco designs.

Art Deco, like the earlier Art Nouveau style, differed in the United States from its European origins in subtle and not-so-subtle ways. Art Nouveau was not a major stylistic influence in America, but the ceramics decorated by women artists at Newcomb College in Louisiana, the furniture designs by Charles Rohlf, and the sensuously curving glass vases of Louis Comfort Tiffany remain exemplars of its American translation. The lamps of Janene A. and Noel F. Hilliard in this survey (plates 14, 15) recall Art Nouveau and the Arts and Crafts movement. Jane Goco's stylized references to floral forms in North Carolina, where she lives, echo Art Nouveau sensuality (plate 12). Albert Paley, internationally respected for his highly stylized forged gates, furniture, and sculpture (plate 27) acknowledged the Spanish Art Nouveau of Antonio Gaudi as an influence on his earliest designs in forged iron in the 1970s. Today he is designing and producing architectural gates, railings, and functional ornament for architecture on a grand scale. Winning a competition to design tree

grates, benches to encircle trees, and lampposts for Pennsylvania Avenue in Washington, D.C., Paley was among the first of contemporary American makers to design in a familiar material, but for an unfamiliar process—cast iron. The diversity and quality of his work have brought comparisons with the great French decorative artist, Hector Guimard. Paley, like Guimard—who designed the entrances to the Paris Metro—has moved from iron as his exclusive material and has designed bronze door hardware to enhance prestigious architecture.

Art Deco furniture in America often substituted plastic and chromium for the ivory and silver that had characterized the style in France in the 1920s. In the American eighties, it is translated even further. Perhaps Anthony Giachetti evokes the luxurious French furniture most successfully (plate 10). The fluted doors of his tall cabinet and the richness of his materials give distinction to his design. His work, like that of others here, builds on Wendell Castle's use of inlays and precious materials in his late 1970s furniture evoking Art Deco styles. Examples here by Dale Broholm (plate 2) and Lee Weitzman (plate 36) also have an Art Deco sensibility in the use of contrasting materials for bold graphic effect. They, like Robert Davis in his Excalibur Spoons (plate 69), and Janet Prip in her Man and Woman Bowl (plate 85), use crisp lines and contrasting materials and colors in ways that evoke the 1920s and thirties. John and Jan Gilmor (plate 47), and Thomas Buechner III (plates 42–44) remind us of Art Deco styling in their glass vases as well.

THE 1930S INSPIRED in other ways. The decade saw the dawning of modernism in Europe and America. Constructivism, the Wiener Werkstatte in Vienna, the Bauhaus in Germany—all have contributed to the American designer's source of inspiration. Marek Cecula draws on the Constructivist use of primary colors and black to decorate his angular tea set (plate 99). Tom Loeser's inventive folding/hanging chair (plate 19) seems to have its origins in Gerrit Rietveld's chairs from Holland. Though Thomas Hucker (plate 16) claims Japanese influence, his dramatic chairs also recall the rectilinear quality of Joseph Hoffman's and Kolomon Moser's Viennese designs—considered by some to emanate from those of Scottish architect Charles Rennie Mackintosh.

The designs of Mackintosh have also inspired Wendy Maruyama and Beth Yoe in their chairs shown here (plates 22, 38). Richard Mafong also acknowledges Mackintosh's Ingram chair as inspiration for his Ingram Bowl and Candlesticks (plate 76, 77). David Tisdale's Tray (plate 89) and Boris Bally's Candle Sculptures and Flatware (plates 65, 66) use early modern ideas aggressively. Vincent and Carolyn Carleton rely on geometric designs and subtle color modulations in their rug—as much a reference to Southwest Indian baskets and Chinese brocades as to European modernism (plate 127).

The twenties and thirties were, as well, the time in which Native American and vernacular/folk art were being rediscovered in America. And they continue to be rediscovered by each new generation. Just as the quilt remains America's quintessential craft tradition, constantly being updated and reinterpreted, other forms of naïve American art have been rediscovered by furniture makers, weavers, and potters.

Daniel Mack's Rustic Wright Chairs are a double spoof (plate 20). Their stylistic origins are the rustic twig furniture found in the Adirondacks of New York State and in other regions of the country. But Mack gives them shapes reminiscent of Frank Lloyd Wright's high-back dining chairs. Does his name for them refer as well to Russel Wright, another famous American designer of the twentieth century?

Vernacular furniture made from recycled materials has inspired Mitch Ryerson to make his child's rocker with a washboard back and clothespin braces (plate 28). And his picture frames, evoking memories of rustic hunting cabins, depict one of the nation's favorite solo pastimes— fishing (plate 29). Tommy Simpson has made a pie safe (plate 31), an anachronism in modern homes more apt to use a freezer and a microwave oven to bring dessert to the table. But this is hardly a reproduction. His unfailing good humor comes across in his use of the characteristic punched-tin panels to depict twelve American "firsts"— the first safety pin, the first dog movie star, the first chewing gum, and so forth.

The nostalgic use of familiar historic forms—sometimes exaggerated or altered—makes Anne Kraus's and Mara Superior's ceramics (plates 110, 119) especially appropriate for pictorial or narrative embellishment. Each deliberately distorts traditional shapes, then decorates them with hand-drawn stories or pictures. This refers not only to American tradition; it recalls the commemorative ceramics traditional to Great Britain, Germany, and other European nations. Both artists studied painting before pursuing ce-

ramics as their medium, and they use that skill well. Sara J. Hotchkiss weaves rag rugs—a pioneer's necessity—but with a contemporary artist's command of graphic design and color (plate 128).

Illusion and strong graphic imagery inspire Karen Casey Burchette, Michael K. Speaker, Wendell Castle, Silas Kopf, Karen Thuesen Massaro, Walter White, Barbara Bauer, Adrian Saxe, and Jenny Lind. All rely on the realistic depiction of familiar objects. Karen Burchette, a graphic artist who has adapted posterlike imagery to furniture made by others to her specifications, sees images boldly. Her chair, its back representing a flattened depiction of the U.S. Capitol dome, is from her own Washington by Design series (plate 3). She, like Miriam Schapiro, Joyce Kozloff, Scott Burton, and other artists who have high visibility in the "fine" arts, has no trouble crossing that invisible line into the decorative arts.

Michael Speaker's vision is also bold, but he renders it in three dimensions. His Red River Steer Desk (plate 32), a masterwork in wood mosaic, is a portrait of a real-life, prize-winning Texas Longhorn steer. It was offered for sale in the 1984 Nieman-Marcus Christmas Catalogue as a unique "His and Hers" selection, calling attention to the unorthodox ways that modern craftsmen may sell their work. The desk is now a prized possession of South Fork Ranch, where exteriors for the television series *Dallas* were filmed.

Wendell Castle (plate 4), one of the most celebrated of modern furniture sculptors, moved away from the organic style of laminated furniture for which he was widely recognized in the 1960s. First, he investigated luxurious French furniture of the 1920s and thirties, using these as source for his elegant tables and cabinets of rich woods, inlaid with ivory, ebony, or sterling silver. His next body of work was almost purely sculptural. Replicas of Queen Anne chairs or other traditional furniture styles were carved, complete with hats, gloves, or other objects resting on them. His newest work is in a gutsier, freer style, using colored stains.

Silas Kopf (plate 18) stands apart from all other American makers in his masterful use of illusionistic marquetry— the technique of creating complex pictures in colored inlaid wood. For years he embellished his handsome furniture with naturalistic flowers rendered in wood inlay. A fellowship awarded by the National Endowment for the Arts enabled him to study marquetry illusion in European museum collections. Since then he has been refining his approach to marquetry, using that time-honored technique to enhance his furniture with contemporary *trompe l'œil* scenes.

Karen Massaro (plate 113) has created a still-life sculpture of porcelain fruit but has given it a purpose. The decorated flat surfaces may be used to serve real fruit. Walter White, Barbara Bauer, and Adrian Saxe have incorporated casts taken from asparagus, conch shell, and eggplant, respectively, in their objects (plates 95, 97, 116). Their flatware and beverage servers, like Jenny Lind's Cat Teapot (plate 111), inspired by the Japanese beckoning-cat figures, recall the fantasy serving pieces that once graced the imperial tables of China and Germany. Saxe has said that he mines the entire history of the decorative arts in his work.

Chinese ceramic traditions have also inspired Shirley Keyes, Donald Sprague, and Richard T. Notkin. Onto her sensuously swelling, undulating vases and covered jars, Keyes has airbrushed a finishing glaze; its soft, grainy texture catches the light like sand dunes in moonlight (plate 109). Sprague's robust stoneware lamp base recalls the form and surface of ancient bronze Chinese drums (plate 33). Notkin has explored the naturalistic, illusionistic references of Chinese Xiching teapots. In the red clay traditional to Xiching wares, he sculpts modern-day narratives. His Cooling Towers Teapot, with its smoke clouds resembling skulls, warns of nuclear disaster (plate 114).

Tom and Elaine Coleman reflect the strong Asian ceramic heritage of the Pacific Northwest where they learned their art. Tom relies on the simplicity of the calligraphic brush stroke to decorate teapots and vessels (plate 102). Elaine carves sensuous forms into hardened porcelain clay, then fires it with a traditional celadon glaze (plate 101).

The late Ruth Lee Kao, born in China but raised and educated in the United States, returned to her homeland with designs for a series of silk pile wall hangings. Made by skilled Chinese artisans in a factory producing opulent rugs, Kao's art reflects her heritage while remaining distinctly American and modern (plate 129).

Japanese influences have guided the hands of Curtis and Suzan Benzle (plate 98) and Thomas Hoadley (plate 108), who have developed stylish applications to the Japanese patterning of colored porcelain clay for their vessels. Ralph Bacerra (plate 96) draws inspiration from Japanese Imari ware; he has reinterpreted both form and decoration in personal, contemporary ways. Dennis Morinaka (plate 125) has looked to Japan for technique, creating stunningly original containers of bamboo, fabric, and wood with surfaces richly embellished with lacquered pattern.

Since the 1970s, Japanese textile techniques have had a strong impact on American fiber artists and their work—especially in traditional patterning methods using dyes.

For example, Lyn Sterling Montagne dyed the weft of her Leaf Rug #2 (plate 131) using the *ikat* method. But, typical of artists' innovations today, she shifted the weft as she wove the twill fabric; she then emphasized the rayon weft diagonals, painting them with fiber-reactive dyes. She also painted the linen surface.

Numerous artists acknowledge their debt to the Orient, but fewer have borrowed from the African continent, though mud-resist dyeing methods are familiar in the modern fiber artist's vocabulary of techniques. Perhaps because African tribal art has become recognized in the West for its style and vitality, the furniture of Judy Kensley McKie—alone in this survey—reminds us of Africa with her bold style in carving animals to decorat or support her tables, chests, and bureaus (plate 23).

McKie's use of surface decoration is one of many explored by contemporary makers. The 1980s have revalued decorated surfaces after years in which the unadorned form seem to define good taste. Today we can appreciate the complexity of Peter Greenwood's Black Lace Tableware, employing Venetian latticinio methods of creating rich patterning within the glass (plate 48). In this era of greater craft specialization, David Boye has made the knife his single specialty. He decorates the blades of these functional forms, making them objects of celebration (plate 68).

Shirley Keyes's use of airbrushing as a glaze application method has already been mentioned (plate 109). Joseph Godwin applies layers of colored slip—clay thinned with water—then carves it away, revealing layers of color in the process (plate 106). John Parker Glick revels in the decorated surface, layering transparent colors for a subtle richness. His Tray (plate 105) shows the continual refinement of the style that has brought him recognition in the last two decades, notably through the commissioning of table settings for the house of the vice president of the United States during the Carter-Mondale administration in the late 1970s.

The 1980s saw the power lathe—fixture of many home workshops—become a tool for artists as the turning of wood bowls was revived. Peter M. Petrochko (plate 126) has taken a different route to creating vessels from richly grained and colorful woods. With a bandsaw, he cuts concentric ovals or other unusual shapes not possible to turn on a lathe, alternates them with contrasting woods, and glues them all together. He then shapes and finishes them, complementing nature's artifice with the artist's ingenuity.

The color of wood is important to Petrochko's work; he uses natural colors rather than dyeing, painting, or lacquering the wood as others do. Color, in fact, is one of the most important components of the new decorative arts. In the 1980s, a singular style with its origins in Milan, Italy, gained world prominence. The Memphis style was a new international style, but it boasted a lone American designer in Peter Shire. Shire's furniture in the Memphis collection carried forward the design ideas embodied in his colorful, sculptural ceramic tea and coffee pots—vivid colors, juxtaposition of unusual shapes, deliberate and provocative jabs at "good taste" by aggressive, seemingly unmatched elements. His Small Scorpion T-Pot (plate 118) exemplifies his own and the Memphis styles, but others have taken up their brilliant new palettes to wash the world with unexpected hues.

S AMUEL A. SHAW (plate 30) has taken his clues from the Memphis line, seeming to draw his lamps and tables in tubular metal. Both Dorothy Hafner (plate 107) and Judith Salomon (plate 115) combine freely imagined colors on forms usually constructed from ceramic slabs. Graceful lines give way to gutsy form. So it is true with the ceramic coffee mugs by Frank Fabens (plate 104), whose sculptural shapes seem almost hacked out of clay. His use of slip casting to produce a line is consistent with production and marketing trends.

Jean-Pierre Hsu, a successful ceramist for years, gave up clay to join his wife, jeweler Carol Shannon Hsu, in working with colorful anodized aluminum. Their serving pieces (plates 74, 75) speak of today, but the 1950s echo beneath their matte surfaces. Kurt Swanson and Lisa Schwartz (plate 61) delight in colored glass and, in addition to their designs named for Vienna, they have developed lamps and other similarly vivid products for their line. Though a "product line" may seem antithetical to handmaking, younger makers like Judy Smilow see their future in designing and making objects in limited quantities, and designing other goods for mass production. Color is absent in Smilow's clear glass plates and tumblers (plates 54, 55), but their floating shapes are another reminder of the 1980s design ideas.

Color and abstract imagery also dominate the work of Susan Stinsmuehlen-Amend (plate 34) and Sid Garrison (plate 121), whose respective media—glass (stained and leaded) and leather—looked quite different in the hands of artists in the past. Stained glass is no longer for windows only; Stinsmuehlen-Amend shows the expressive possibilities of her medium for folding screens that can function as independent art objects in a room. Garrison moves far away from the belts and bags so ubiquitous in the 1960s, forming, tooling, and inlaying his vibrantly colored skins into stunning compositions.

Though color may govern much of this new wave of 1980s decorative arts, not all artists choose it as their principal design tool. The creation of pure forms—clear in their profiles, often relying on subtle surface texture to reveal the quality of material—seems the interest of furniture makers John Bickel (plate 1), Jeff Kellar (plate 17), and Sam Maloof (plate 21), ceramists Lea Embree (plate 103) and James D. Makins (plate 112), and glass artist Stephan J. Cox (plates 45, 46). Perhaps it is the durability of the Scandinavian modern design ethic that governs their work, or the ideals of the Arts and Crafts movement.

The ideals of American craftsmen are indeed diverse, but diversity is inherent in the nature of our people and the forms of their expression. What lies ahead in a new century? Maybe a renewal of interest in the ruggedness of frontier crafts and traditional rural chairs, jugs, and rugs. Certainly manufacturers have responded to each new design inspiration, whether it has been country French, High Tech, or the American Southwest. American craftsmen, competing in the race for the consumer dollar, will follow such trends. But they will also lead, for they are well aware that the temptation to create only for the tastes of others can leave their work barren of personal meaning and energy. American crafts have survived war and depression; I believe that they will survive fashion, too.

Furniture and Lighting

1 **John Bickel** *b. 1920*
Walnut Branch Chair *Designed 1982, made 1984*
Walnut: steam-bent, laminated, traditional mortise-tenon joinery
46 × 22 × 24

Dimensions are in inches, height × width × depth

Unless otherwise noted, the object has been loaned by the artist

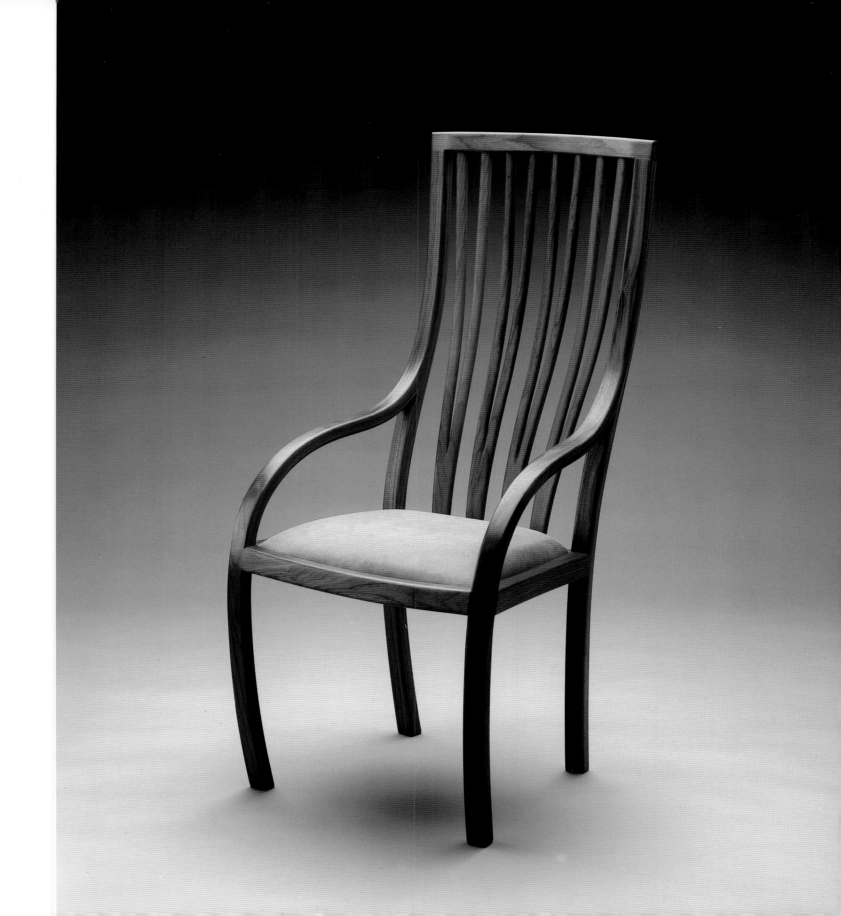

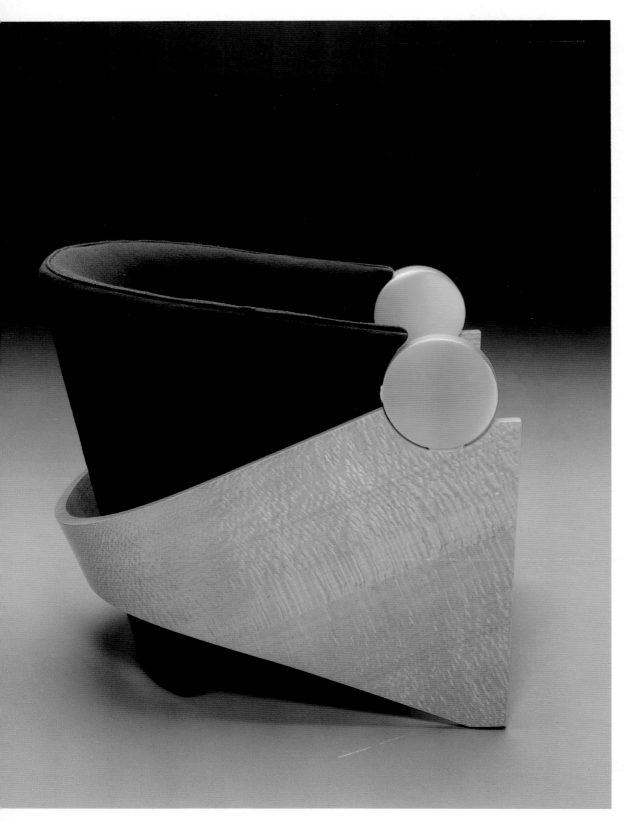

2 **Dale Broholm** *b. 1956*
Easy Chair *1983*
Lacewood veneer, bent plywood, painted maple, ash
30 × 26 × 26
Dean Powell photograph

3 **Karen Casey Burchette** *b. 1946*
Capitol Chair, Washington by Design *1986*
Wood, resin, lacquer
48 × 19 × 23
Courtesy of Karen Burchette for Country Garden, Ltd.

4 **Wendell Castle** *b. 1932*
Untitled Humidor *Designed 1988, made 1988–89*
Cherry, bleached lacewood, rosewood veneer,
mahogany veneer, Cuban cedar liner
12½ × 27 × 11¾
Courtesy of Caligari Corporation, New York, NY
Michael Galatis photograph

5, 6, 7 **Keith Crowder** *b. 1962*
Shaman Lights *Designed 1987, made 1989*
Mixed media: carved, lashed
Redhead *75 × 10 × 9*
Münch *80 × 10 × 9*
Skull *75 × 10 × 9*

8 John Dodd *b. 1954*
Cylindrical Compliment *Designed 1980, made 1988*
Walnut, beeswing narra: laminated, veneered, turned
48 × 12 × 12

9 Christopher R. Ellison *b. 1959*
Demilune *1988*
Copper, steel, glass: welded, brazed, sandblasted
32 × 48 × 18

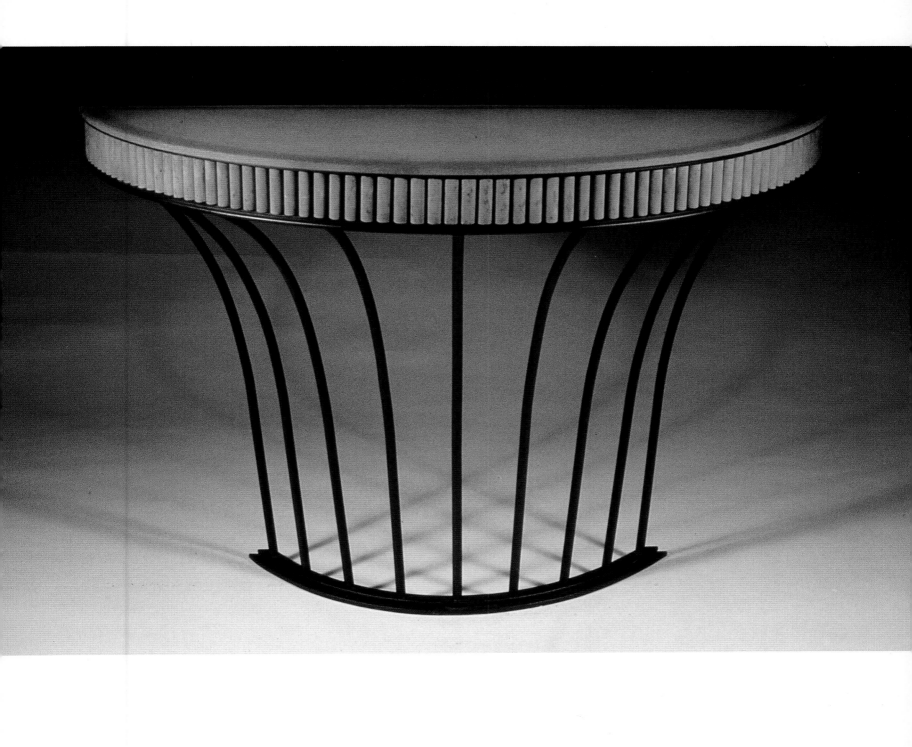

10 **Anthony Giachetti** *b. 1944*
Fluted Cabinet #882 *Designed 1986, made 1988*
Curly mahogany, rosewood, Swiss pearwood inlay
65 × 32 × 19
Stretch Tuemmler photograph

11 **Glasslight, Inc. (Joel Bless, Candace Luke-Bless,
Daniel Gaumer, Matthew Seasholtz, Kathleen Gaumer)**
Round Drawing Lamp *Designed 1986, made 1989*
Glass: free-blown base, glass powders and glass drawing on surface
24 × 18 × 13

12 **Jane Goco** *b. 1935*
Magnolia Mantel Form *1980*
American walnut: laminated, carved
54 × 84½ × 3¼

13 **Peter Handler** *b. 1947*
Garçon Serving Cart *Designed 1987, made 1988*
Aluminum: machined and anodized; glass
22½ × 32 × 30

14 **Janene A. Hilliard** *b. 1952*
Black and Pink China Lamp *1988*
Fused and soldered glass tiles, cast bronze
17 × 15 × 15
G. Post photograph

15 **Noel F. Hilliard** *b. 1948*
Umbrella Lamp *Designed 1985, made 1988*
Twisted and slumped glass, cast bronze
60 × 23 × 23

16 **Thomas Hucker** *b. 1956*
Two Side Chairs *Designed 1986, made 1988*
Pearwood, plywood, lacquer
Each 29 × 44 × 22
Courtesy of Franklin Parrasch Galleries, New York, NY

17 **Jeff Kellar** (*with* **Judy LaBrasca**) *b. 1949*
Rocking Chair *Designed 1980, made 1988*
East Indian rosewood, black cotton tape: solid wood and bent lamination
40 × 25 × 39

18 **Silas Kopf** *b. 1949*
Typewriter Desk
Mahogany, satinwood: marquetry
46 × 46 × 24
Courtesy of Viretta King

19 **Tom Loeser** *b. 1956*
Folding Chairs *Designed 1982, made 1988*
Maple, plywood, stainless steel, paint
Each 34 × 28 × 22

20 **Daniel Mack** *b. 1947*
Rustic Wright Chair *Designed 1987, made 1988*
Red maple, sugar maple, upholstered seat
62 × 21 × 17
Bob Hanson photograph

21 **Sam Maloof** *b. 1916*
Double Rocker *1988*
Hardrock fiddleback maple
47 × 42 × 47
Gene Sasse photograph

22 **Wendy Maruyama** *b. 1952*
Mickey Mackintosh Chair *Designed 1982, made 1988*
Zolotone over poplar
60 × 24 × 16

23 **Judy Kensley McKie** *b. 1944*
Table with Dogs *1979*
Mahogany: laminated and carved; glass top
34 × 62 × 18
Bob Hanson photograph

24 **Rick Melby** *b. 1952*
Orbit *Designed 1986, made 1989*
Textured sheet glass
13 × 13 × 5

25 **Richard Scott Newman** *b. 1946*
Fluted Chair *1982*
Pearwood, bronze ormolu, silk upholstery
36 × 19 × 19
Courtesy of The Collection of Anne and Ronald Abramson

26, 27 **Albert Paley** *b. 1944*
[Not illustrated] Plant Stand *1988*
Mild steel: forged and fabricated; slate: carved
50¼ × 20½; top 12⅞ dia.
Courtesy of Fendrick Gallery, Washington, DC,
and New York, NY

Plant Stand *1988*
Mild steel: forged and fabricated; slate
50½ × 19 × 17
Courtesy of Fendrick Gallery, Washington, DC,
and New York, NY
D. James Dee photograph

28 **Mitch Ryerson** *b. 1955*
Washboard Rocker *1986*
Maple, cherry, washboard, soap box labels
26 × 12 × 21

29 **Mitch Ryerson** *b. 1955*
Man of the Woods (Ernie) *1987*
Pear, wenge, hand-colored photograph
23½ × 15 × 1

30 **Samuel A. Shaw** *b. 1954*
Floor Lamp *Designed 1986, made 1987*
Brass, copper, wood: fabricated
41 × 10 × 20

31 Tommy Simpson *b. 1939*
The 1st Pie Safe *1985*
Wood, tin, photographs
71 × 22 × 19
Courtesy of Joanne Rapp Gallery/The Hand and the Spirit,
Scottsdale, AZ
Collection of Dr. and Mrs. Dennis Brydon

32 Michael K. Speaker *b. 1946*
[*Not touring*] Red River Steer Desk *1984 (detail)*
(See also Frontispiece)
Gonzalo albes, ebony, maple: traditional joinery
54 × 84 × 32
1984 Nieman-Marcus Christmas Catalogue photograph

33 Donald Sprague *b. 1946*
Lamp *1988*
Stoneware: reduction-fired, cone 10
24 × 20 × 20
Jim Piper photograph

34 Susan Stinsmuehlen-Amend *b. 1948*
Pro Rata Lyricism Screen *Designed 1987, made 1988*
Handblown roundels, etched and leaded glass in ash frame
91 × 96 × 1½

35 **Bob Trotman** b. 1947
Dancing Table (with Dice) Designed 1981, made 1988
Maple: traditional joinery; lacquer
25½ × 13 × 13
John S. Payne photograph

36 **Lee Weitzman** b. 1954
Spiral Table Designed 1984, made 1989
Wood, lacquer
29 × 19
Courtesy of Hokin Kaufman Gallery, Chicago, IL

37 **Barry Yavener** *b. 1955*
Neo-Empire Table with Mirror *1985*
Black bean wood, marble, lacquer, gold leaf, brass, aluminum
Table 36 × 40 × 17; mirror 38 × 38 × 2
Courtesy of Franklin Parrasch Galleries, New York, NY
Evan H. Sheppard photograph

38 **Beth Yoe** *b. 1947*
Chinese/Mackintosh Chair *1987*
Ash, brass, leather, lacquer
57 × 20 × 16

Glass Tableware and Decorative Accessories

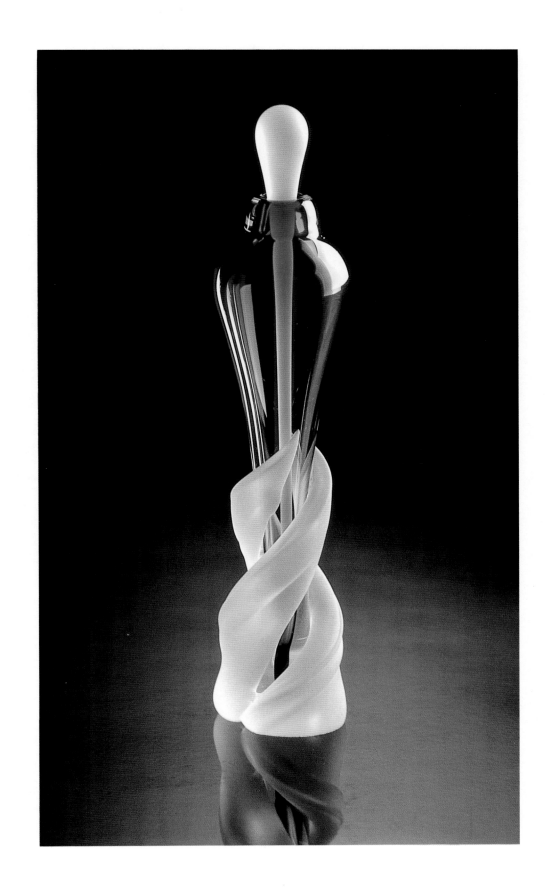

39 **Matthew Buechner** *b. 1957*
Emerging Form Perfume Bottle *Designed 1980, made 1989*
Glass: blown, with sandblasted base and stopper
7 × 1½
Courtesy of artist, Thames Street Glass House, Newport, RI
John Wells photograph

40 **Matthew Buechner** *b. 1957*
Feathered Trail Perfume Bottle *Designed 1982, made 1989*
Glass: blown, with molten colored glass applied to surface in stripes, then pulled
5½ h
Courtesy of artist, Thames Street Glass House, Newport, RI

41 **Matthew Buechner** *b. 1957*
Gold/Silver Leaf Perfume Bottles *Designed 1982, made 1989*
Glass: blown, 23k gold and silver applied to surface
5 h
Courtesy of artist, Thames Street Glass House, Newport, RI

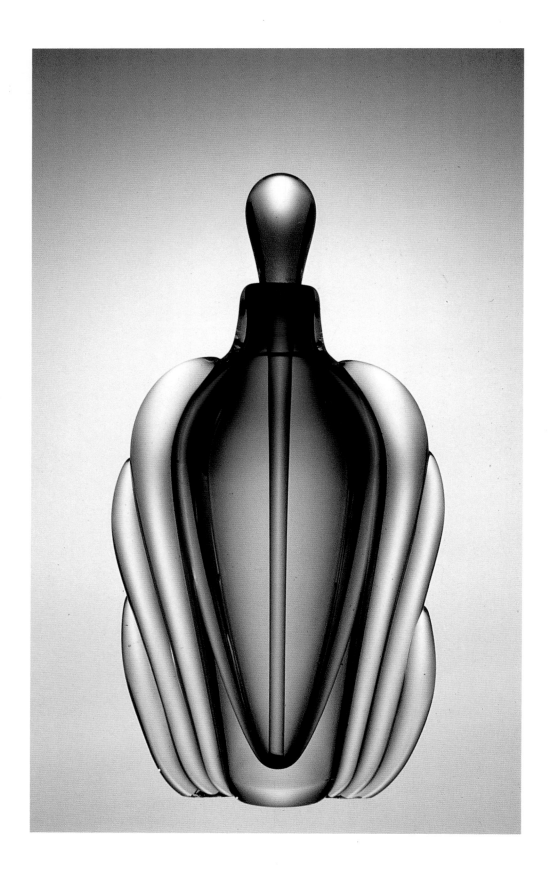

42 Thomas Buechner III *b. 1954*
Multibit Perfume Bottle *Designed 1982, made 1989*
Glass: blown
4½ × 3

43 Thomas Buechner III *b. 1954*
Multibit Vase *Designed 1984, made 1989*
Glass: blown
12 × 6 × 4

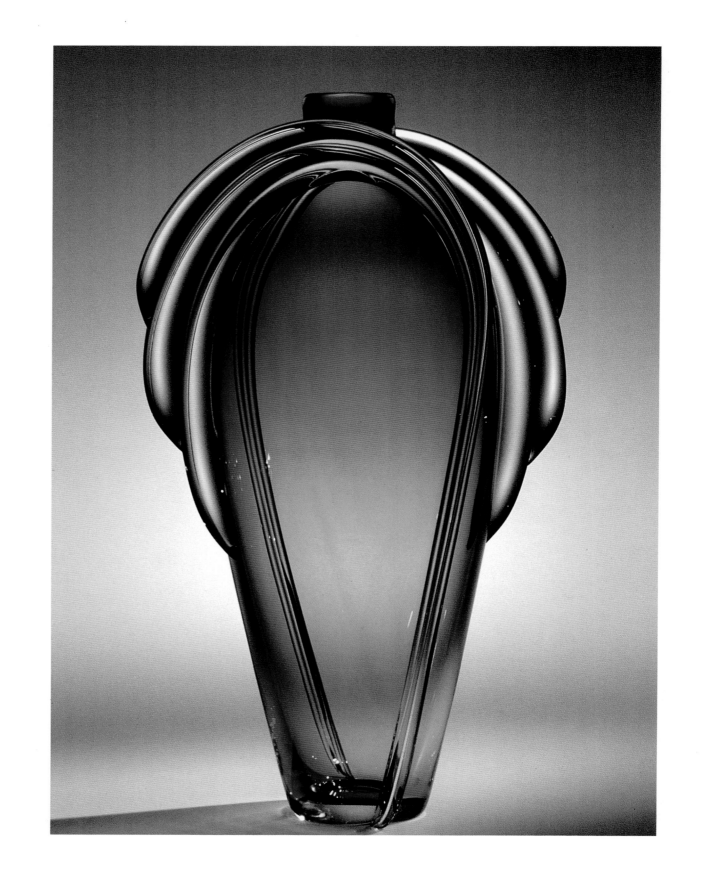

44 Thomas Buechner III *b. 1954*
Tellurian Perfume Bottle *Designed 1988, made 1989*
Glass: blown, lampworked Pyrex stopper
8 × 3½

45 Stephan J. Cox *b. 1956*
Carved Shallow Bowls *1987*
Glass: blown, sandblasted, diamond-saw cut, wheel-ground
3 × 5¾, and 4 × 7

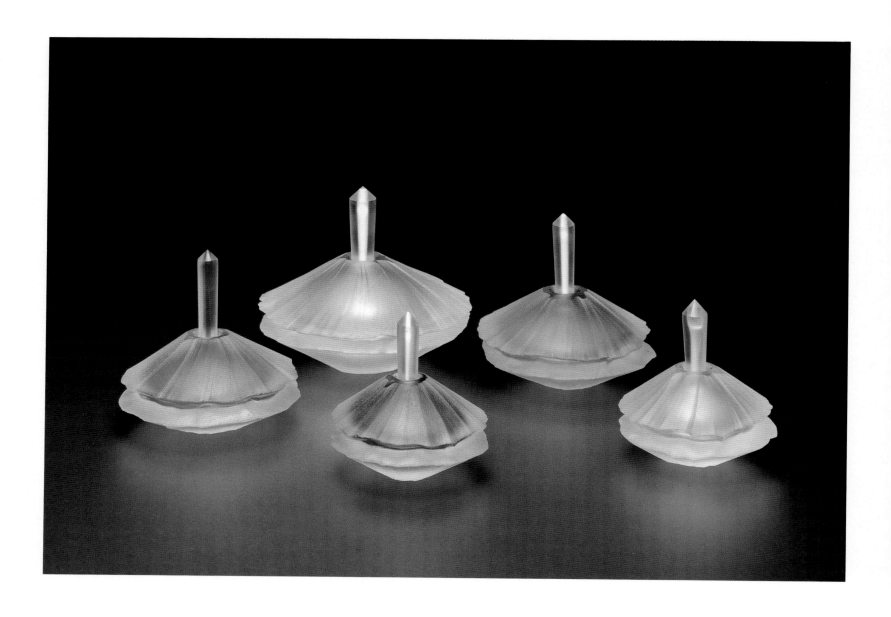

46 **Stephan J. Cox** *b. 1956*
Carved Squat Perfume Bottles *1987*
Glass: blown, with applied color, sandblasted,
diamond-saw cut, wheel-ground
2 × 2½, and 3½ × 5

47 **John** *and* **Jan Gilmor** *b. 1950, 1952*
Conical-base Cylinder *1982*
Glass: blown, sandblasted
13 × 4¾

48 Peter Greenwood *b. 1960*
Black Lace Tableware *1986*
Glass: blown, latticinio
Tallest goblet 7 h, plate 10 dia.

49 James Harmon *b. 1952*
Sushi Plate #101 *Designed 1985, made 1987*
Glass: cast
5 × 8 × 2
Courtesy of artist, Harmon Design Group, Philadelphia, PA
Lori Sewiuk photograph

50 Steven Maslach *b. 1950*
Fractured Dichroic Bowl *1988*
Crystal: cast, blown, cut, laminated with variable color filters
11 h × 10 dia.

51 Steven Maslach *b. 1950*
Latticinio Marble Goblet *Designed 1979, made 1988*
Blown glass with latticinio marble in stem
8 h

52 **Steven Maslach** *b. 1950*
Latticinio Flutes *Designed 1981, made 1988*
Blown glass with cane work
9 h

53 **Steven Maslach** *b. 1950*
Gold Lustre Goblet *Designed 1978, made 1988*
Crystal containing silver and cobalt, iridized surface
9 h

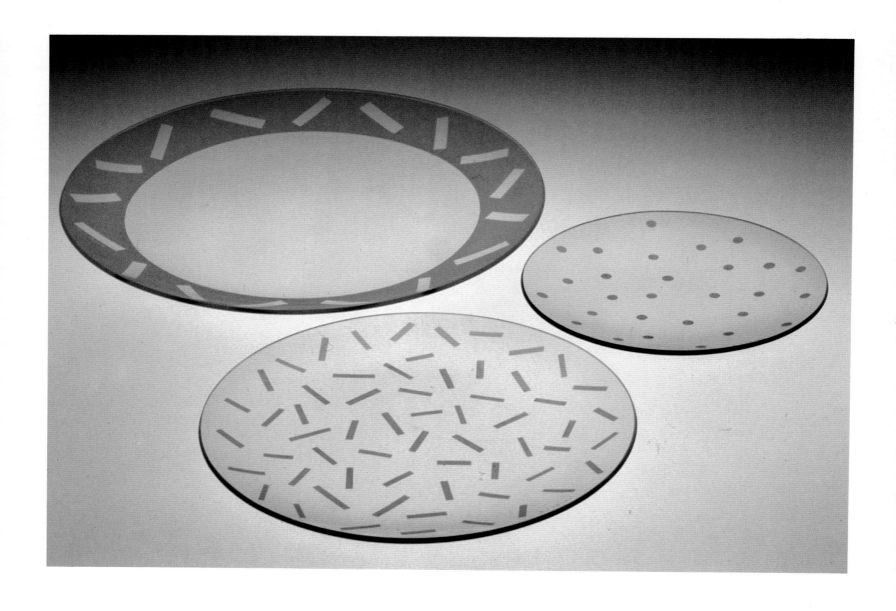

54 **Judy Smilow** *b. 1958*
Dots and Dash Plate Set *Designed 1985, made 1989*
Glass: frosted and bent
12, 9, and 7 dia.

55 **Judy Smilow** *b. 1958*
Mixed Patterned Glasses *Designed 1987, made 1988*
Frosted glass
3½ and 3⅛ dia.

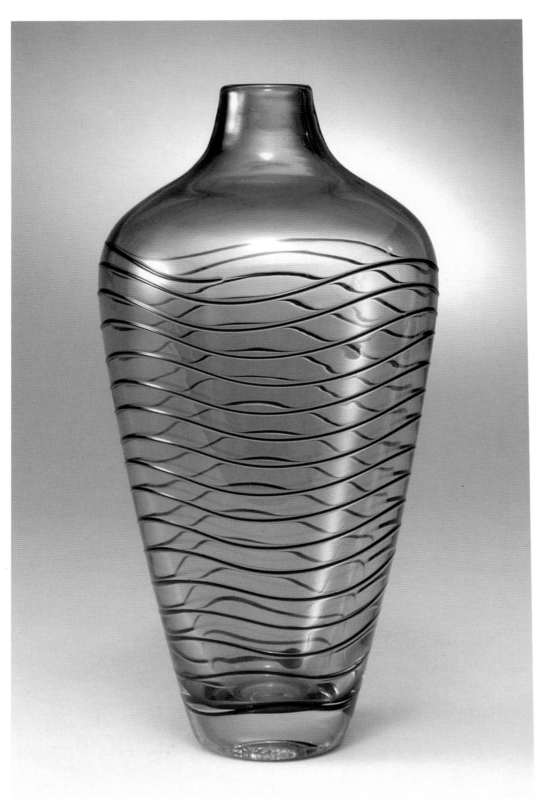

56 **Stephen Smyers** *b. 1948*
Wave Vase (Manhattan) *Designed 1980, made 1981*
Blown glass
11¼ × 5½

57 **Stephen Smyers** *b. 1948*
Vienna Plume Wine Goblets *Designed 1985, made 1988*
Blown glass
8¼ × 3½
Michele Maier photograph

58 Stephen Smyers *b. 1948*
London Dot Wine/Champagne *Designed 1985, made 1989*
Blown glass
8½ × 3½
Michele Maier photograph

59 Stephen Smyers *b. 1948*
Paris 10 oz. Wine Goblet *Designed 1980, made 1988*
Blown glass
8¾ × 3¼

60 **Stephen Smyers** *b. 1948*
Corfu Cocktail Set *Designed 1982, made 1988*
Blown glass
Glasses 4¼ × 3½, mixer 9¼ × 3½, stirrer 12
Michele Maier photograph

61 **Kurt Swanson** *and* **Lisa Schwartz** *b. 1958, 1959*
Vienna Vase and Two Vienna Bowls
Blown glass
Vase 15 × 8 × 5, bowls 8 × 6 × 6

62 **Paul J. Stankard** *b. 1943*
Environmental Paperweight *Designed 1986, made 1988*
Lampworked glass
2 × 3¼
Courtesy of Patricia Stankard

63 **Walter White** *b. 1949*
Suggestive Gesture *Designed 1986, made 1988*
Glass: blown into copper matrix
10½ × 10
Robert Vinnedge photograph

64 Craig Zweifel *b. 1944*
Round Vessel, TW Pattern *1985*
Blown glass with crystalline silver surface, applied dark glass overlays
6¾ × 6 × 6

Metal Tableware and Decorative Accessories

65 **Boris Bally** *b. 1961*
Flatware *Designed 1987, made 1988*
Sterling silver: lost-wax cast, stamped, fabricated, and riveted; ebony
Lengths: 12, 9, 8½, 8, 7¼
Courtesy of Archetype Gallery, New York, NY

66 **Boris Bally** *b. 1961*
Stacked Pentagon Candle Sculptures *1988*
Brass, silver, gold plate: pressed and fabricated, tied cold joints; slate
5 tier 6¾ × 3¾; 3 tier 4½ × 3¾
Courtesy of Archetype Gallery, New York, NY

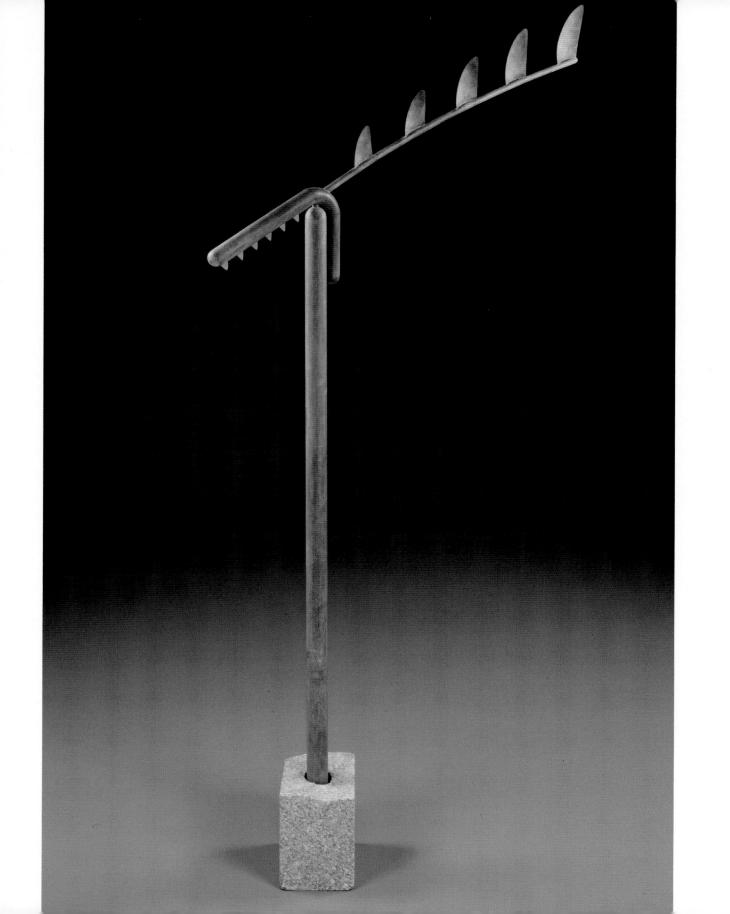

67 **Jonathan Bonner** *b. 1947*
Weathervane *Designed 1988, made 1989*
Copper, granite
85 × 55 × 8

68 **David Boye** *b. 1941*
Eight-inch Chef's Knife *1988*
Cast dendritic 440c stainless steel blade
12 × 2 × ¾

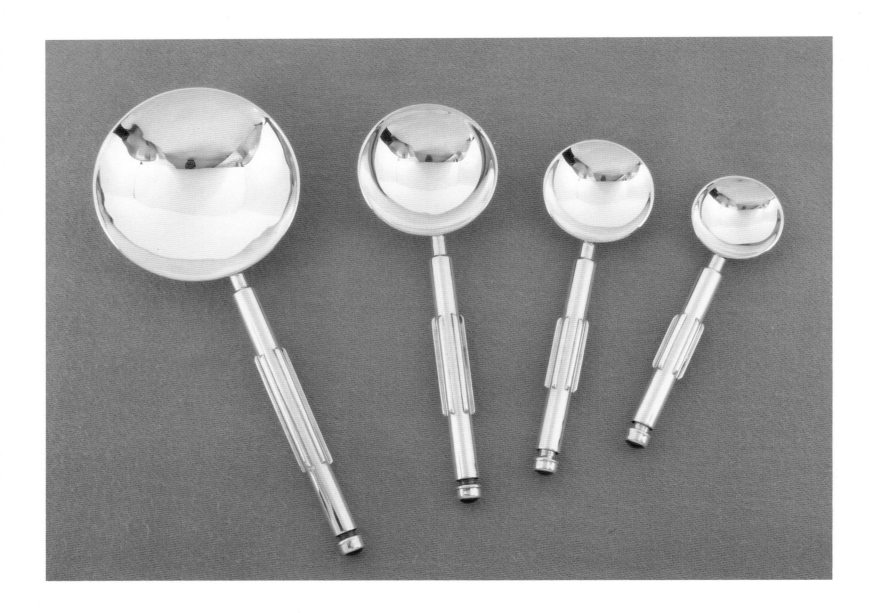

69 **Robert Davis** *b. 1944*
Excalibur Spoons *Designed 1985, made 1986*
Sterling silver: fabricated, raised bowls
5 × 2, 4 × 1⅜, 3½ × 1¹⁄₁₆, 3 × ⅞
Courtesy of Jean Sampel

70 **Fred Fenster** *b. 1934*
Kiddush Cup *1988*
Raised and fabricated pewter
9 × 6

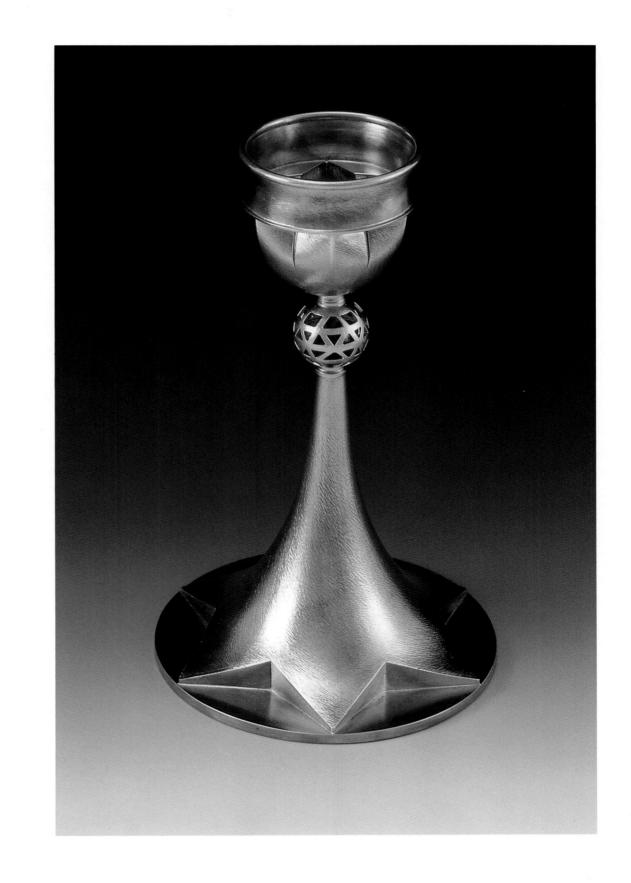

71 **Fred Fenster** *b. 1934*
Salt and Pepper Shakers *1984*
Raised and constructed pewter
3 dia.
F. J. Hurley photograph

72 **Pat Flynn** *b. 1954*
Pewter Drinking Beakers *Designed 1976, made 1989*
Pewter, sterling silver, gold-plated interior
3½ × 2½ × 2½
Courtesy of Susan Cummins Gallery, Mill Valley, CA
Alexander Caster photograph

73 **Gary S. Griffin** *b. 1945*
Garden Gate *1985*
Steel: hammered, welded, carved
70 × 92 × 18

74 **Carol** *and* **Jean-Pierre Hsu** *b. 1952, 1953*
Basket *Designed 1985, made 1988*
Aluminum, nylon, rubber: textured, anodized, assembled
2½ × 16 × 10

75 **Carol** *and* **Jean-Pierre Hsu** *b. 1952, 1953*
Serving Bowl *Designed 1987, made 1988*
Aluminum and rubber: formed, anodized, assembled
6 × 11½ × 11½

76, 77 **Richard Mafong** *b. 1942*
Ingram Bowl *1987*
Silverplated brass: spun and constructed
8 × 15
Ingram Candlesticks *1987*
Silverplated brass
9 × 5
Gary Bogue photograph

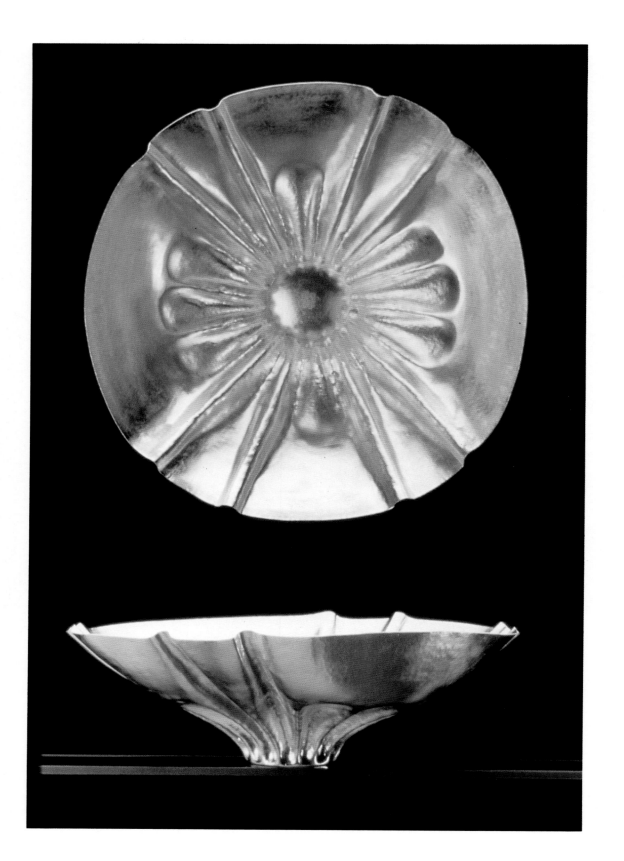

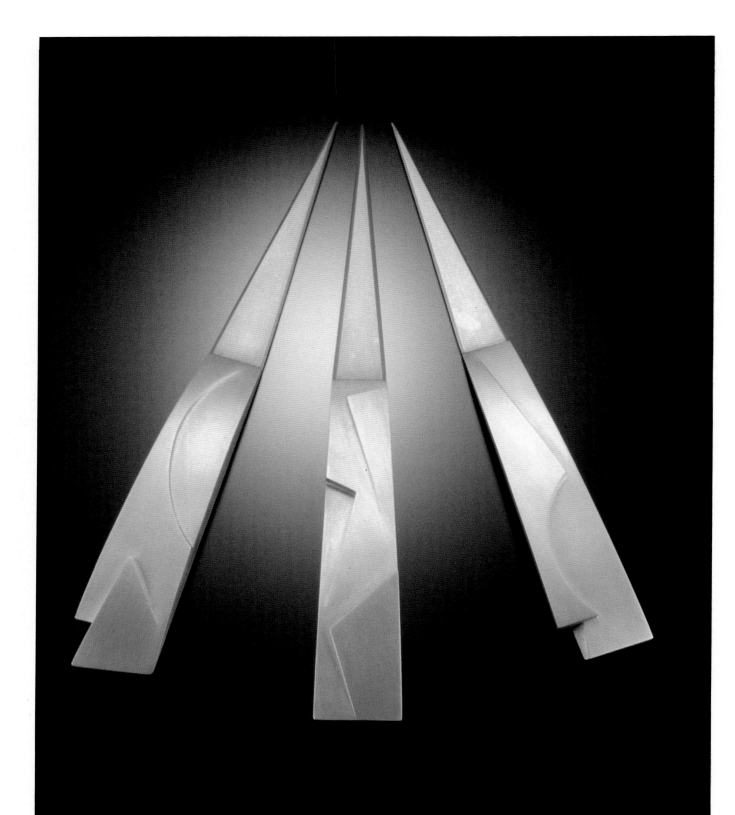

83 Tony Papp *b. 1961*
Three Letter Openers *1988*
Sterling silver and nickel: hollow forms constructed from sheet
9 long
Courtesy of Archetype Gallery, New York, NY
Ralph Gabriner photograph

84 Ronald Hayes Pearson *b. 1924*
Flatware Prototypes *1980*
Silverplated brass: fabricated, forged
Lengths: 9½, 7¾, 7⅜
D. Klopfenstein photograph

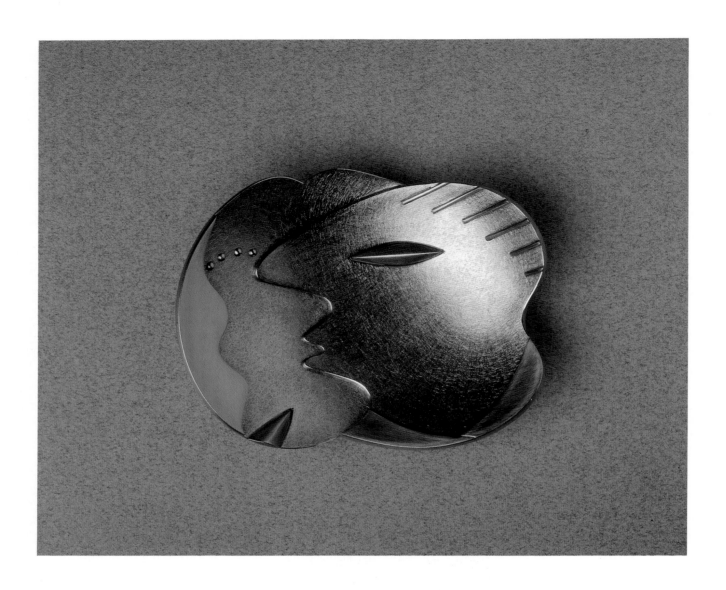

85 **Janet Prip** *b. 1950*
Man and Woman Bowl *1983*
Pewter, brass: fabricated
4½ × 4½
Courtesy of John and Karen Prip

86 **Claire Sanford** *b. 1958*
Black Wrapped Vessel *1985*
Fabricated copper, sulphur patina
12 × 6 × 6

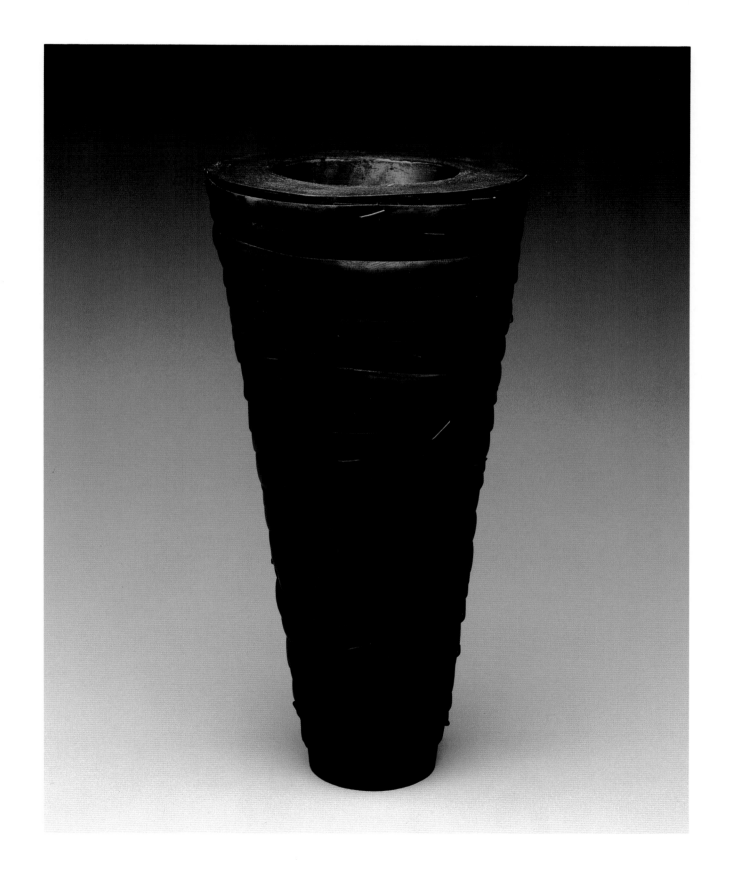

87 **Peggy Simmons** *b. 1950*
Triangular Teaball *Designed 1980, made 1987*
Sterling silver, ivory, 14k gold
8½ × 2 × 1

88 **Peggy Simmons** *b. 1950*
Teardrop Teaball *1982*
Sterling silver, 14k gold
9½ × 1½ × 1½

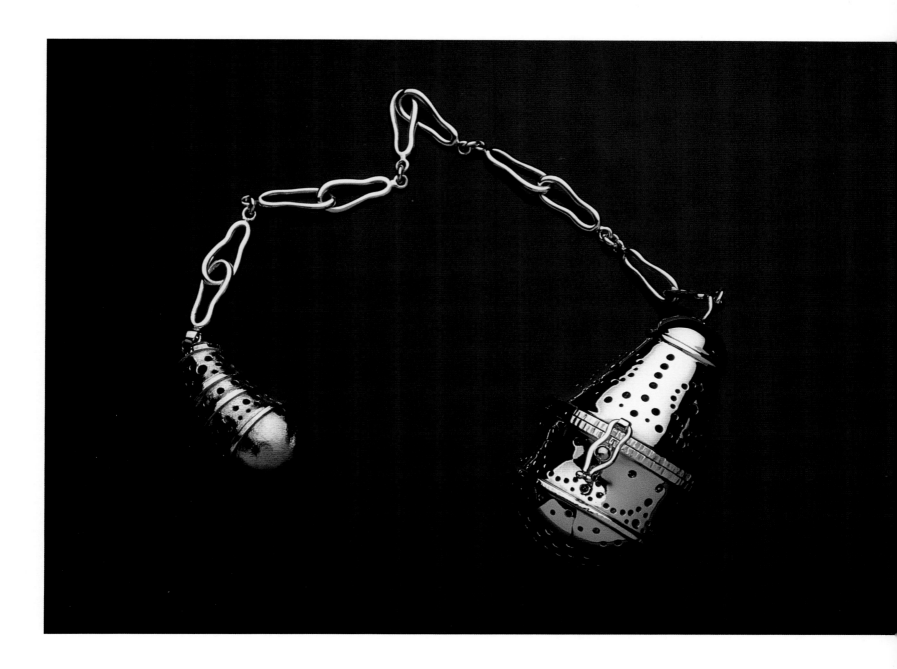

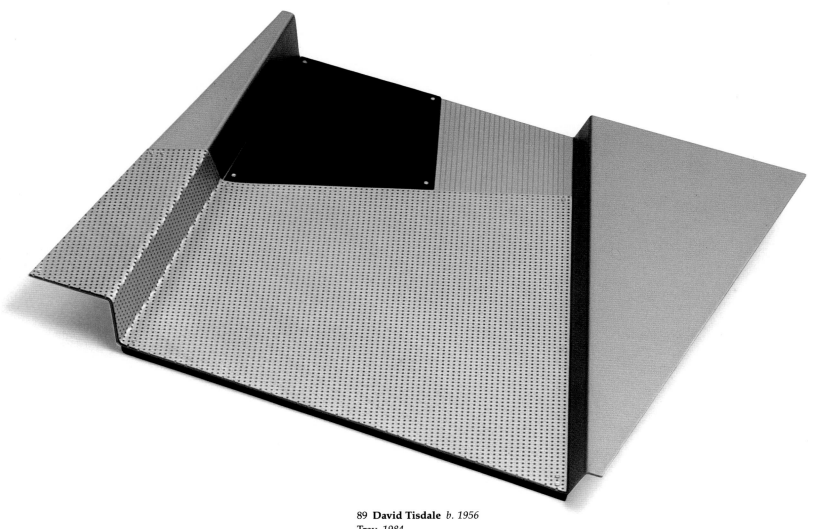

89 **David Tisdale** *b. 1956*
Tray *1984*
Anodized aluminum, acrylic, stainless steel screws
9 × 10½ × 1¼

90, 91, 92, 93 **David Tisdale** *b. 1956*
Two Napkin Rings *Designed 1986, made 1988*
Anodized aluminum: riveted
2½ × 1½ × 1
Two Demitasse Spoons *Designed 1986, made 1988*
Anodized aluminum: fabricated, riveted
4¼ × ⅞ × ¼
Two Butter Knives *Designed 1986, made 1988*
Anodized aluminum: riveted
6¼ × ⅞ × ⅛
Two Coasters *Designed 1986, made 1988*
Anodized aluminum, acrylic
3 × 3 × ¼

94 **Raychel Wengenroth** *b. 1960*
Ladle *1982*
Sterling silver and niobium: forged, raised, and fabricated
12 × 4½ × 8
Courtesy of Richard and E. Lou Wengenroth

95 **Walter White** *b. 1949*
Asparagus Flatware *Designed 1979, made 1981*
Sterling silver: cast and forged; stainless steel blade
Teaspoon 6⅞, tablespoon 7¾, knife 10, luncheon fork 7½, dinner fork 8⅜
Courtesy of Fendrick Gallery, Washington, DC, and New York, NY
Jim Cummins photograph

Ceramic Tableware and Decorative Accessories

96 Ralph Bacerra *b. 1938*
Covered Stacked Container *1980*
Porcelain
12 × 6
Courtesy of Leatrice and Melvin Eagle

97 **Barbara Bauer** *b. 1949*
Queen Conch Shell Teaset *Designed 1980, made 1986*
High-fired porcelain: slip-cast, 14k gold and mother-of-pearl luster glazes
Teapot 9 h, tray 10 long
Courtesy of "This Day and Age," private collection, ME

98 **Curtis** *and* **Suzan Benzle** *b. 1949, 1950*
Silent Song *1988*
Porcelain: refractory stains
8 × 18 × 3

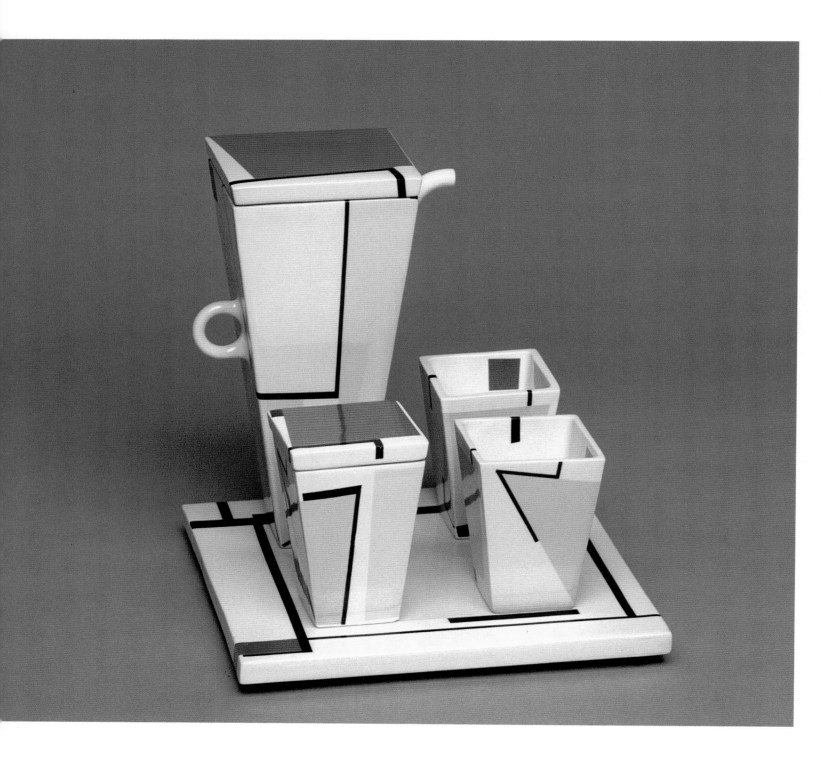

99 **Marek Cecula** *b. 1944*
Graphic Set *Designed 1983, made 1989*
Porcelain: slip-cast, assembled, glazed; decals: multi-fired
Teapot 7 h, tray 7 × 7
Courtesy of Contemporary Porcelain Gallery, New York, NY
Bill Waltzer photograph

100 **Margaret Chatelain** *b. 1949*
Dominoes Dinnerware and Platter *Designed 1986, made 1989*
White earthenware: slip-cast, airbrushed underglaze design, clear surface glaze
Platter 19 long, plates 10 and 8
Tayo Gabler photograph

101 **Elaine Coleman** *b. 1945*
Teapot *1989*
High-fired porcelain: carved, celadon glaze
12 × 7

102 **Tom Coleman** *b. 1945*
Porcelain T-Pot *1988*
Porcelain: oxide decoration
10 × 9

103 **Lea Embree** *b.1934*
Berry Bowls *1988*
High-fired porcelain: textured, unglazed outer surface
Large bowl 2½ × 6¾, small bowls 1⅜ × 4¼

104 **Frank Fabens** *b. 1959*
Two Tall Cups and Saucers *1988*
Slip-cast porcelain
4 × 5

105 John Parker Glick *b. 1938*
Tray *1988*
Stoneware: slab-built, glaze-painted, reduction-fired
17½ × 19¾ × 2½
Dirk Bakker photograph

106 Joseph L. Godwin *b. 1947*
Vessel *Designed 1984, made 1987*
Porcelain: carved through slip
10 × 9
Werner Hauser photograph

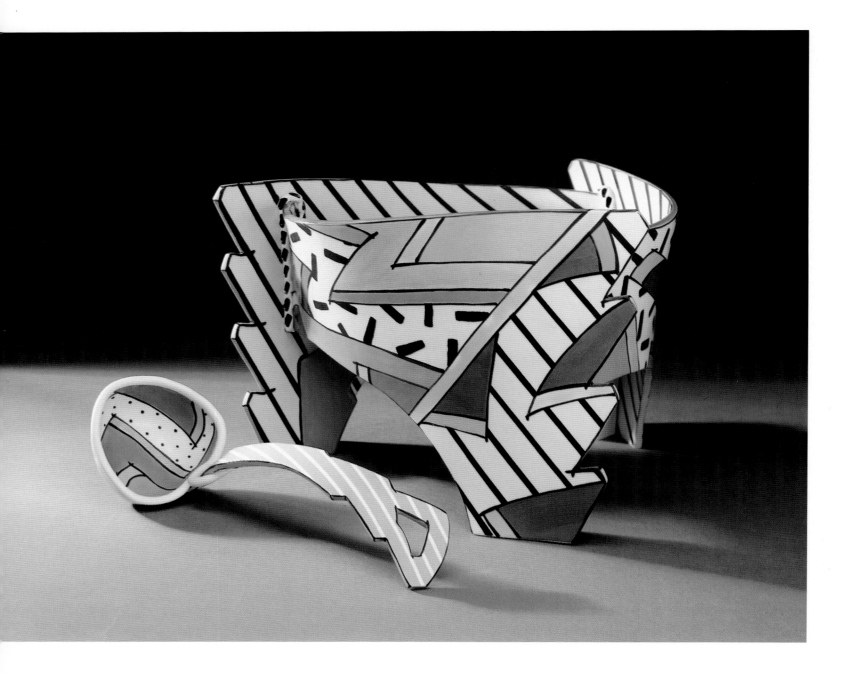

107 **Dorothy Hafner** b. 1952
Flic Flac Punchbowl with Ladle 1988
Porcelain: underglaze decoration
8¾ × 12¾ × 12¾

108 **Thomas Hoadley** b. 1949
Nerikomi Vessel 1988
Colored porcelain: nerikomi *technique*
7 × 9 × 11½
Sandy McNay photograph

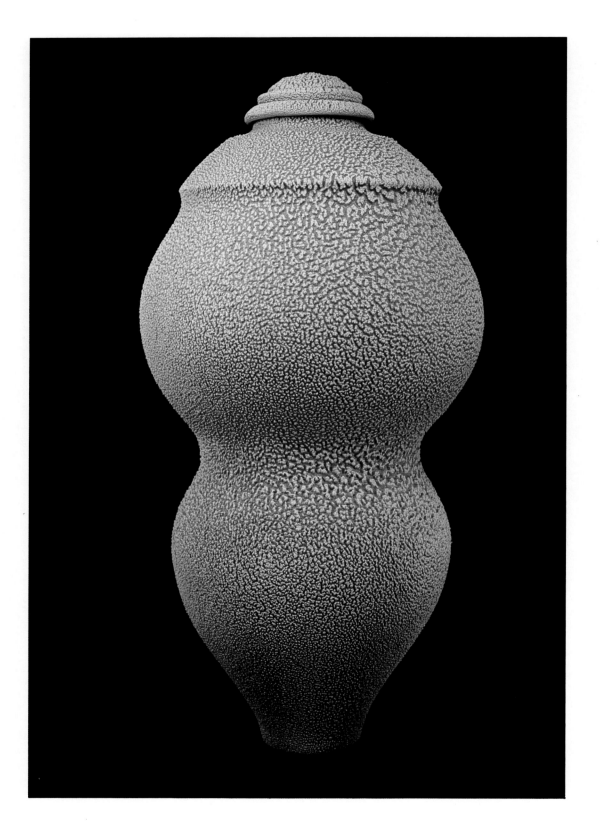

109 **Shirley Keyes** *b. 1942*
Sensations *1988*
White stoneware: spray-glazed with stains and oxides
22 × 10½ × 10½

110 **Anne Kraus** *b. 1956*
Lovers Cup *1988*
Whiteware with glazes
4 × 7½
Courtesy of Garth Clark and Mark DelVecchio
Tony Cunha photograph

111 **Jenny Lind** *for* **Animals & Co.** *b. 1942*
Cat Teapot *1983*
Slip-cast porcelain: painted with engobes
8½ h
Courtesy of anonymous lender

112 **James D. Makins** *b. 1946*
Dinnerware *Designed 1973, made 1989*
Porcelain: wheel-thrown
Place setting 8 × 24 × 18

113 **Karen Thuesen Massaro** *b. 1944*
Paired Fruit Servers II *1988*
Slip-cast porcelain: black underglaze decoration
4 × 17 × 9½
Lee Hocker photograph

114 **Richard T. Notkin** *b. 1948*
Cooling Towers Teapot #3B *1983*
Stoneware
6 × 9 × 3¾
Courtesy of Daniel Jacobs

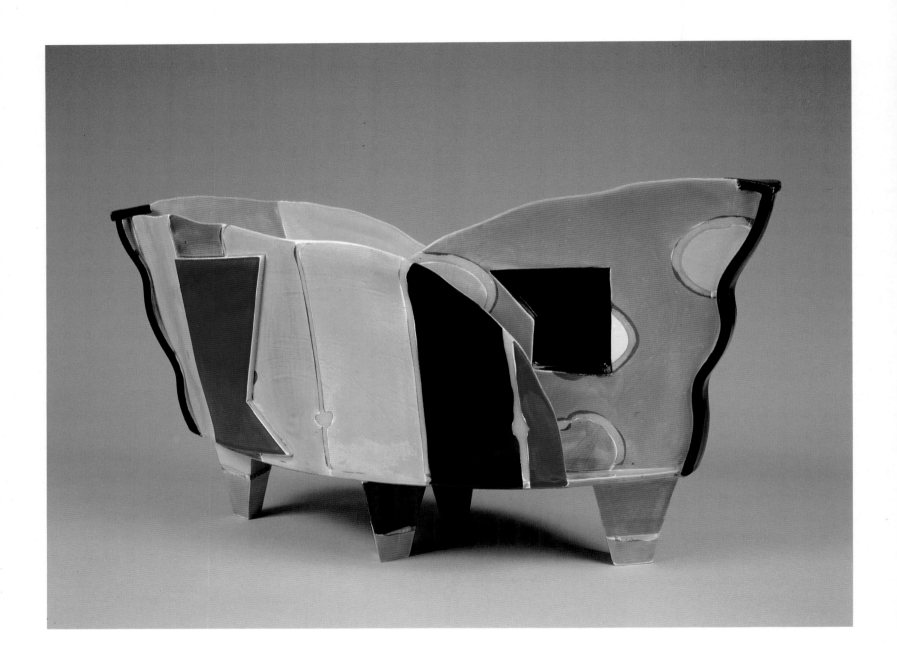

115 **Judith Salomon** *b. 1952*
Orange Envelope Vase *1987*
Whiteware: handbuilt, low-fired
10 × 18 × 9
Bruce Chelefsky photograph

116 **Adrian Saxe** *b. 1943*
Eggplant Teapot *1982*
Porcelain with glazes
7½ × 6¼
Courtesy of The Saxe Collection

117 **Kaete Brittin Shaw** *b. 1945*
Teapot, Anemone Series *1987*
Porcelain: handbuilt, inlaid colors
17 × 14 × 5
Bob Hanson photograph

118 **Peter Shire** *b. 1947*
Small Scorpion T-Pot *1984*
Whiteware
10¼ × 18½ × 10¼
Courtesy of William and Anne Traver
Eduardo Calderon photograph

119 **Mara Superior** b. 1951
Cocoa Pot *Designed 1987, made 1988*
Slab-constructed porcelain
18 × 15 × 7

120 **Robert G. F. Woo** b. 1948
Covered Serving Dish *Designed 1985, made 1987*
Thrown stoneware, saturated iron liner glaze, celadon
exterior glaze: cobalt, iron, and titanium slip decoration
7 × 10 × 10
Courtesy of anonymous lender

Wood and Leather Containers and Clocks

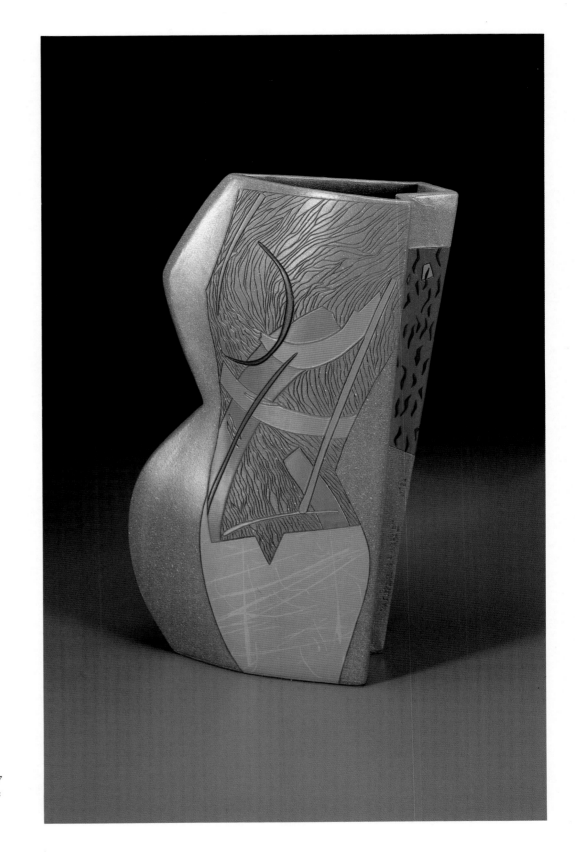

121 **Sid Garrison** *b. 1954*
A Surprise and a Miracle *Designed 1985–86, made 1987*
Wet-formed laminated leather: incised, painted with acrylics
18 × 11 × 5
Larry Fleming photograph

122 Po Shun Leong *b. 1941*
Landscape Container *1988*
Cherry burl, wenge, mahogany, Hawaiian koa: bandsaw-carved, layered
19 × 22 × 6

123 Robert G. McKeown *1930–1989*
Bubinga Desk Clock *Designed 1980, made 1988*
Bubinga, with cast polyester resin inserts
9½ h
Courtesy of Lee H. McKeown

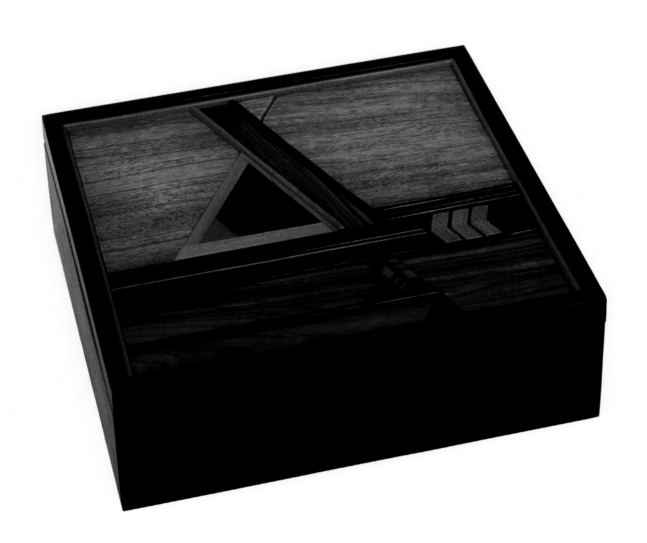

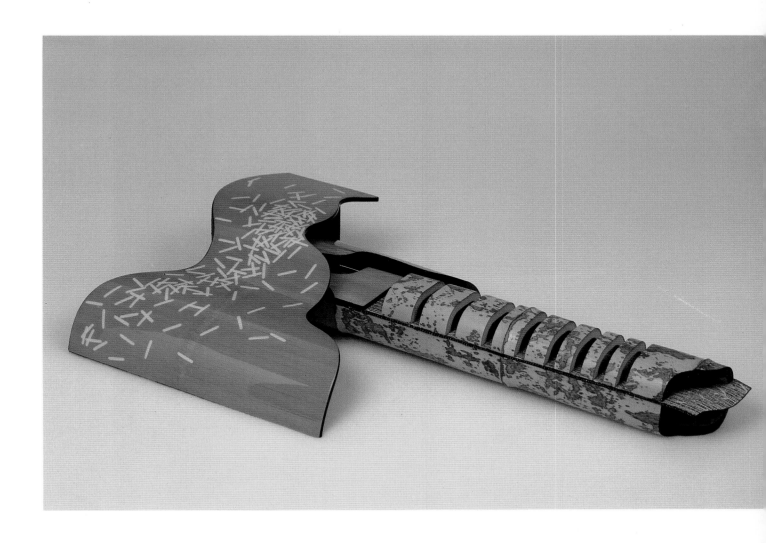

124 **Robert G. McKeown** *1930–1989*
Tellurian Jewelry Box *Designed 1985, made 1988*
Wood, with accents of pigmented resin
3¼ × 8½ × 8½
Courtesy of Lee H. McKeown

125 **Dennis M. Morinaka** *b. 1945*
Made in Oakland *Designed 1986, made 1986–88*
Laminated bamboo, French pearlized paper, Japanese ikat cloth, brass powder, lacquer
4½ × 23 × 13
Courtesy Garth Clark Gallery, New York, NY, and Los Angeles, CA

126 **Peter M. Petrochko** *b. 1948*
Landscape Series Bowl *1986*
Brazilian rosewood, African padouk: bandsawn, hand-carved, laminated
14 × 14 × 20
Courtesy of Pam and John King, Buffalo Gallery, Alexandria, VA

Rugs

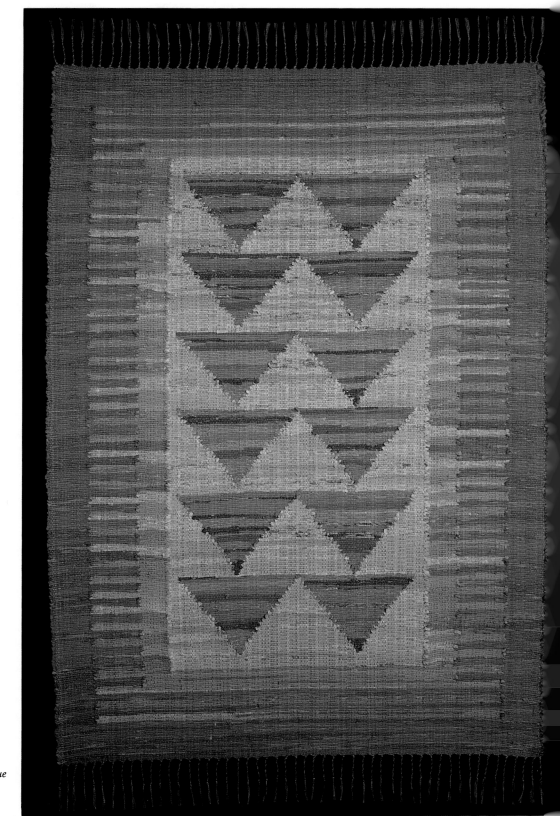

127 Carolyn *and* **Vincent Carleton** *b. 1956, 1951*
Parallax *Designed 1983, made 1989*
Worsted wool, Belgian linen: handwoven reversible flatweave
72 × 108

128 Sara J. Hotchkiss *b. 1951*
Blue Sunrise *Designed 1987, made 1989*
Perle cotton warp, cotton fabric strips: handwoven, tapestry technique
54 × 76

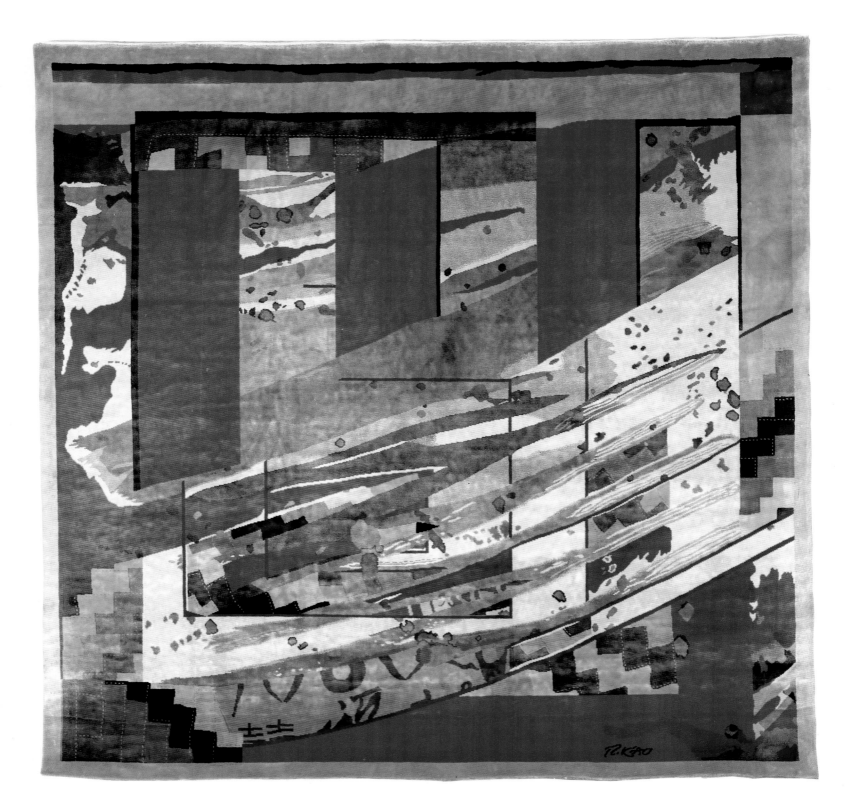

129 **Ruth Lee Kao** *1933–1985*
Silk Tapestry (Untitled #6) *Designed 1985, made 1986*
Silk: handwoven, hand-knotted pile
84 × 84
Courtesy of the artist's children

130 **Beth Minear** *b. 1939*
Photo Finish *1987*
Wool weft, linen warp: handwoven
79 × 45
Courtesy of Elizabeth and Charles Agle
Edward Owen photograph

131 **Lyn Sterling Montagne** *b. 1953*
Leaf Rug #2 *1988*
Linen weft, rayon and linen warp: ikat *dyed,*
twill handwoven, painted
84 × 53

Index of Artists